WHAT YOUR COLLEAGUES ARE SAYING . . .

"'Bell-to-bell teaching' can be full of variety and delight, and Molly Ness offers teachers of all grade levels a huge assist here with her trove of concrete, wide-ranging activities to enhance and lighten the hard work of any class. My favorites are the Reading Graffiti and Sticky Sort, and her conversational style leaves even a seasoned teacher reminded of old favorites like 'Hink Pinks' and recommitted to use every moment we have with our young ones. I will be recommending this book widely."

—**Gretchen Bernabei**, Author of *Text Structures From Poetry* and *Text Structures From Fairy Tales*

"Have you been looking for sensible ways to enrich and energize your transition times? Stop searching and simply turn these pages! In *Every Minute Matters*, Molly Ness has carefully curated a menu of literacy-linked ideas that will engage learners and maximize instructional time. Once you start using Ness's ideas, your students will surely be asking for more."

—**Maria Walther**, Traveling Teacher, Literacy Consultant, and Author of *The Ramped-Up Read Aloud*

"Molly Ness is a fierce advocate for literacy, dedicated to amplifying and improving the learning lives of children everywhere. In *Every Minute Matters*, Ness continues this vital mission. I greatly appreciate that this smart, practical resource is centered on a common challenge: it often feels like there's never enough time. The included explanation of 'time audits' helps readers prepare to rethink current practices and uncover hidden minutes. Ness then provides forty practical learning routines to make each 'found' minute matter. Perhaps what I most appreciate is the joy and playfulness inherent in each research-supported suggestion! The flexible instructional practices detailed throughout the book are a powerful antidote to worksheets and workbooks. Additionally, in the Minute Mentor feature, Ness points readers in the direction of where they can find more, read more, learn more, and do more. I am confident this multifaceted resource will be well-loved by hardworking educators as they rethink and reimagine the infinite opportunities for meaningful, integrated literacy learning that could be tucked into every day."

—**Pamela Koutrakos**, Author of *Word Study That Sticks* and *The Word Study That Sticks Companion*

"As usual, Dr. Ness clearly organizes and explicitly describes strategies and activities to create a literacy-rich classroom culture. Specifically, I appreciate the activities that are targeted for transitions, as I am interested in how teachers negotiate lost instructional time during transitions. Dr. Ness provides great ideas to turn this lost time into fun yet meaningful instructional time. Another great book!"

—**Douglas DiStefano, PhD**, Kindergarten Teacher Springhurst Elementary, Dobbs Ferry, NY

"Molly Ness has written a book that belongs in every teacher's hands. Through both cited and her own research, she reminds us of the importance of instructional minutes. Maybe even more important, she challenges readers to consider how they spend their time, and she provides authentic, relevant, and fun activities that are so much more than time fillers. Every activity has a specific purpose and explanation, and she has designed them to fit into and enhance the structure of our students' learning lives. This book is not only valuable and practical for enhancing instruction, it will bring fun and joy into classrooms!"

—**Melanie Meehan**, Author of *Every Child Can Write*

"*Every Minute Matters* is loaded with practical activities that teachers can use to insert meaningful literacy instruction into those precious minutes otherwise lost to transitions. But this is so much more than an activity book. It's a guide to reflecting upon how we use our students' most precious resource: time."

—**Lauren Prosoff,** Author of *EMPOWER Your Students* and
Two-for-One Teaching

"*Every Minute Matters* is a tremendous resource for educators looking to enhance their literacy curriculum and provide purposeful instruction. Dr. Molly Ness has expertly curated an engaging catalog of games and activities to support the development of a child's reading, writing, speaking, and listening skills. I've already found a few favorites my students love!"

—**Gary Wellbrock, PhD,** Early Childhood Educator at PS347
The American Sign Language and English Lower School in Manhattan

EVERY MINUTE MATTERS

40+ ACTIVITIES FOR **LITERACY-RICH** CLASSROOM TRANSITIONS

MOLLY NESS

FOR INFORMATION:

Corwin
A SAGE Companyy
2455 Teller Road
Thousand Oaks, California 91320
(800) 233-9936
www.corwin.com

SAGE Publications Ltd.
1 Oliver's Yard
55 City Road
London EC1Y 1SP
United Kingdom

SAGE Publications India Pvt. Ltd.
B 1/l 1 Mohan Cooperative Industrial Area
Mathura Road, New Delhi 110 044
India

SAGE Publications Asia-Pacific Pte. Ltd.
18 Cross Street #10-10/11/12
China Square Central
Singapore 048423

Acquisitions Editor: Tori Bachman
Editorial Development Manager: Julie Nemer
Associate Content Development Editor: Sharon Wu
Production Editor: Amy Schroller
Copy Editor: Megan Markanich
Typesetter: Hurix Digital
Proofreader: Rae-Ann Goodwin
Indexer: Integra
Cover and Graphic Designer: Scott Van Atta
Marketing Manager: Deena Meyer

Printed in the United States of America

Library of Congress Cataloging-in-Publication Data
Names: Ness, Molly, author.
Title: Every minute matters [Grades K-5] : 40 activities for literacy-rich classroom transitions / Molly Ness.
Description: First edition. | Thousand Oaks, California : Corwin Press, Inc., [2020] | Series: Corwin literacy. | Includes bibliographical references.
Identifiers: LCCN 2020017439 | ISBN 9781544382449 (paperback) | ISBN 9781071818251 (epub) | ISBN 9781071818275 (epub) | ISBN 9781071818305 (ebook)
Subjects: LCSH: Reading (Elementary)—Activity programs. | Critical thinking—Study and teaching (Elementary)—Activity programs.
Classification: LCC LB1573 .N425 2020 | DDC 372.4—dc23
LC record available at https://lccn.loc.gov/2020017439

This book is printed on acid-free paper.

20 21 22 23 24 10 9 8 7 6 5 4 3 2 1

CONTENTS

Visit the online companion at
resources.corwin.com/everyminutematters
for printables to use with some of these activities. The
online companion also contains suggestions for adjusting
activities for distance learning and family play.

GUIDE TO LITERACY-RICH EXPERIENCES

Activity	Related Literacy Skills (Speaking, Listening, Reading, Writing)	Specific Subskills	When You Might Incorporate This Activity	Page #
Rotate Your Writing	Writing	Written responding to a prompt	Start of Day	22
Reader's Notebook Tours	Reading	Responding to text, engaging in conversation about reading		24
Library Love	Reading, Speaking, Listening	Previewing and selecting texts		28
Be a Book Matchmaker	Reading, Writing	Persuasive writing about a text		29
"I Wonder" Writing	Writing	Generating questions, promoting curiosity		32
Beach Ball Bonanza	Listening, Speaking	Following directions, engaging in conversation, responding to classmates		36
Laughing Through Rereadings	Reading, Speaking	Building fluency		38
Read, Record, Reflect	Writing	Building fluency		40
Book Tasting	Reading	Previewing and selecting texts		44
Go Fish	Reading, Speaking	Following directions, engaging in conversation, responding to classmates		48
Concentration	Writing	Building word recognition and automaticity		52
Lining Up With Literacy	Listening, Speaking	Building phonological awareness	Transition Time	54
I Spy	Listening, Speaking	Using phonological awareness and sight word recognition		56
Category Chain	Listening, Speaking	Building working memory through phonological awareness games		58
Ghost Writing	Writing	Improving handwriting		60
Build a Word	Listening, Speaking, Writing	Using oral cues to promote spelling		62
Classroom Charades	Listening, Speaking	Incorporating movement and theater to act out literacy-based clues		64
Telephone	Listening, Speaking	Promoting attentive listening to deliver a message to classmates		66
Would You Rather?	Listening, Speaking	Constructing a persuasive verbal argument		68

Activity	Related Literacy Skills (Speaking, Listening, Reading, Writing)	Specific Subskills	When You Might Incorporate This Activity	Page #
Hink Pinks	Reading	Building phonological awareness and vocabulary	Any Time	70
Human Hungry Hippos	Reading	Reading and responding to phonological awareness clues or sight word instruction		74
Spelling Connect Four	Reading	Building spelling patterns		76
Vocabulary Vase	Listening, Speaking	Using vocabulary words in expressive language		78
Book Pass	Reading, Speaking	Previewing and selecting texts		80
Parking Lot	Listening, Speaking, Writing	Generating questions		82
Sink or Spell	Listening, Speaking ,Writing	Reinforcing spelling		84
Headbands	Talking, Reading	Revisiting familiar vocabulary terms		88
Twister	Listening, Speaking, Reading	Following directions, engaging in sight word recognition		90
Letter Formation	Writing	Incorporating kinesthetic movement into handwriting		92
Sight Word Search	Reading	Drawing attention to sight words in everyday text		94
Letter Tile Table	Reading, Writing	Encouraging spelling and wordplay		96
Tower Tumble	Speaking, Listening	Reviewing vocabulary and scaffolding conversation		98
Checkers	Speaking, Listening	Incorporating terms to generate sentences		100
A to Z About	Reading, Writing	Synthesizing essential terms in relation to a general topic	End of Day	102
Sticky Sort	Reading, Writing	Building connections between topic-themed key terms		106
Reading Graffiti	Reading, Writing	Identifying essential phrases from text		108
Jot Lot	Writing	Sketching to promote text connections		110
Wordoodle	Writing	Reinforcing the spelling and meanings of vocabulary and spelling words		112
Wordo	Reading, Writing	Generating quick sketches to increase vocabulary understanding and retention		114
Character Cards	Reading, Writing	Brainstorming key terms related to topics		118
Categories	Writing	Thinking categorically and generating ideas		122
Character Chats	Reading, Writing	Producing writing from a character's perspective		126
Blackout Poetry	Reading, Writing	Borrowing essential text phrases to generate poetry		128

ACKNOWLEDGMENTS

We don't accomplish anything in this world alone...and whatever happens is the result of the whole tapestry of one's life and all the weavings of individual threads from one to another that creates something.

—Sandra Day O'Connor

As I worked on the final stages of this book, our world was turned upside down from the COVID-19 pandemic. Social distancing and self-quarantining became our norms. In the blink of an eye, schools were shuttered, and teachers scrambled to transform instruction into online formats—with very little advanced time or preparation. I marveled at teachers' heroic efforts to reach their children and to engage them in this new learning space. My profound respect and deep admiration goes to every teacher who poured their heart, creativity, and passion into making this scary time a bit more manageable for our students.

Love and gratitude go to those who offered encouragement, ideas, and childcare as I wrote this book. My most sincere thanks go to Mom and Dad. Tori Bachman, my writing is stronger because of your wisdom and keen eye. Cornelius Minor, I'm lucky to call you a friend. Thank you to my professional colleagues who have devoted their lives to ensuring that all children experience the joy of lifelong reading—my International Literacy Association (ILA) and National Council of Teachers of English (NCTE) friends, my End Book Deserts network (much gratitude to Duane!), the entire Corwin team, my former doc students, and the book nerds at Penguin Random House. Thank you to the Oak Tree women for the cheerleading—especially to Jo Bryan for her photography. And my most sincere thanks extend to the friends who made the dark days of COVID19 a bit brighter—Liz, Andrea, Doug, Donna, Susan, the #pRYEde women, and John.

PUBLISHER'S ACKNOWLEDGMENTS

Corwin gratefully acknowledges the contributions of the following reviewers:

Juli-Ann Benjamin
Instructional Coach/Assistant Principal
Newark Public Schools
Newark, NJ

Patrick Harris
Teacher
Southfield, MI

INTRODUCTION
SO MUCH TO DO, SO LITTLE TIME

When I picked up my third-grade daughter from school the other day, she said, "Mr. Allen is the best teacher, but there's one thing I don't like about him." She explained that her class was the last to report to the lunchroom; though all five third-grade classrooms had lunch at the same time, her class didn't pack up for lunch before the lunch bell. "The other third graders start packing up 5 minutes before the bell," she whined.

Upon hearing this, I did the happy dance. My daughter had the good fortune of having a bell-to-bell teacher. By avoiding the temptation of letting his students begin a premature pack up, Mr. Allen optimized every precious instructional minute. By making the most of every minute in the school day, he conveyed that his students' time was too valuable to waste. Remember the old slogan for Maxwell House coffee? Commercials declared it "good to the last drop." Mr. Allen created classroom time that was good to the last minute. Mr. Allen exemplified the words of Donalyn Miller (2009), who wrote the following in her wildly popular *The Book Whisperer*:

> With instructional time at a premium in every classroom, we cannot afford to waste any of it. (p. 55)

If you've picked up this book, my hunch is that you strive to make the most out of every minute of your instructional day, too. But let's face it: Time is both a real and significant concern. Elementary teachers face a daunting list of content to cover, life skills to impart, e-mails to answer, meetings to attend, and on and on. Time is a real challenge, and there never seems to be enough of it.

MAKING THE MOST OF OUR TIME BY EXAMINING WHAT WE HAVE

The word *busy* is ubiquitous in schools, and time is our most valuable resource. Most teachers I know cite a lack of time as their major obstacle in classroom instruction. None of us has the power to create more minutes in the school day or more school days in the year. But we can be effective and efficient with our time. In the popular psychology book *168 Hours: You Have More Time Than You Think* (Vanderkam, 2010), the author advises us to treat each of our 168 hours in a week as a blank slate, filling up each day of the week with only the most deserving things. Bates and Morgan (2018) extended this idea into classroom literacy instruction, challenging teachers to conduct time audits of their literacy blocks. In listing each instructional practice and its allotted time, we can begin a reflective process and adjust our instructional time to better fit the needs of our students. In Part One of this book, I've included space for you to do a time audit of your instruction (modified from Bates & Morgan, 2018; Brinkerhoff & Roehrig, 2014).

As you conduct a time audit with authenticity and honesty, you'll note times in your instructional day ripe for redesign. I also suspect that many of us will be surprised by how much time is not maximized—time diverted by distractions or rambling student questions, time lost to transitions or bathroom trips, and even unexpected open time that catches us off guard. My research (Ness,

2011, 2016) confirmed this hunch! In over 3,000 minutes of direct classroom observations, I observed 285 minutes of transition. This category included times students took out and put away materials, shifted to new activities, filed in and out of the classroom, and so on. That equals a staggering 12% of instructional time. Imagine what gains your students could make with authentic literacy instruction or tasks during that 12% of time!

A Closer Look at Lost Minutes in the Instructional Day

In their 2014 book, Brinkerhoff and Roehrig report on a time audit conducted by classroom teacher Ms. Rodriguez. They list the following lost minutes that "perpetuated themselves, like weeds in a garden" (Brinkerhoff & Roehrig, 2014, p. 9):

22 minutes standing in line to use the bathroom
+
5 minutes of taking attendance
+
6 minutes to line up to exit the classroom for specials
+
6 minutes to line up and gather items for lunch
+
5 minutes of putting things away
+
10 minutes of managing supplies

= 1 hour of misspent time (or 15% of the school day) …
= More than 100 hours in one school year …
= More than 3 weeks of wasted instructional time!

Sobering Statistics on Lost Instructional Time

- According to Fisher (2009), students spend less than half the time allocated for learning engaged in rigorous cognition.
- Brinkerhoff and Roehrig (2014) point out pervasive time wasters:
  1. Inefficient classroom management
  2. Lessons that aren't aligned to target learning objectives
  3. Lessons that don't engage students in higher-level thinking
- Teachers report that they spend only two-thirds of their time teaching (Morton & Dalton, 2007).
- A 2000 study on an urban school district showed that in 330 minutes of the school day, only 280 minutes were allotted toward actual instruction (Smith, 2000). This same study found an average rate of noninstructional time (the percentage of lesson time that classes spent on noninstructional activities) of 23% for elementary teachers.
- A 1998 report from Chicago Public Schools (Smith, 1998) notes that the expectation is for 300 minutes of daily instruction; the number is actually closer to 240 minutes. They found an average rate of 23% of noninstructional time observed in elementary classrooms. This results in an average annual yield of close to 500 hours of instruction as opposed to the intended 900 hours.

Teachers are busy people in school, there's no doubt. Outside of school, though, teachers have children to raise, relationships to nurture, bills to pay, pets to tend to, meals to prepare, hobbies to enjoy, places to visit, Netflix to binge, and on and on. Do you coach a team or lead a club? There goes more of your time! Do you commute? Are you pursuing graduate classes, certification requirements, or continuing education units? How about a second job to make ends meet or save for something special? Simply put, you're busy—your time is precious across the day and evening.

With so much already to do, the last thing we need is added work. If you spend your free time searching for resources to add to your instructional materials, rest assured that you are not alone. A 2018 survey by K–12 Market Advisors revealed that teachers spend 7 hours per week searching for instructional resources (both free and paid-for) and another 5 hours per week creating their own instructional materials. According to EdReports.org, teachers are heading online to search for ways to supplement their curriculum, with the following self-reported statistics:

- Ninety-seven percent of teachers use Google to supplement their curriculum.
- Eighty-five percent of teachers use Pinterest to supplement their curriculum.
- Seventy-nine percent of teachers use Teachers Pay Teachers to supplement their curriculum.

Do you really have time for that?

WHY YOU NEED THIS BOOK

I've written this book to honor two realities: (1) your instructional time is precious and how you use it affects student learning, and (2) you are busy, and you don't have time to scour the Internet for shiny new ideas. The purpose of this book is to maximize the learning potential of every moment in the classroom—from the second that students enter in the morning to the final bell. *Every Minute Matters* **provides literacy-rich activities to optimize transitional times and minimize lost instructional minutes.** You'll open this book searching for ways to make the most of your instructional day, but en route you will begin critical reflections about your use of time and your instructional priorities.

The literacy-rich activities in this book are not meant to detract from the curriculum, program, or approach that comprises your literacy block. In no way do I intend to replace the effective language arts instruction that already occurs. Instead, I have written this to help you become magicians of time (à la Hermione Granger and her Time-Turner!). After reflecting about your use of instructional time with the framework presented in the next chapter, you may begin to shift your priorities. Perhaps you realize that your morning minute has exceeded the intended 15-minute time frame, and you've got an additional 4 minutes. What literacy-rich experience could your students have here?

While this book is not intended to be a classroom management manual, its ideas may likely lead to improvements in your students' behavior, motivation, and focus. Research confirms that when teachers minimize transitional time, off-task behavior decreases as literacy achievement and student engagement increase (e.g., Codding & Smyth, 2008; Day, Connor, & McClelland, 2015). As we make the most out of every instructional moment, our students are more likely to be on task, engaged, and successful in their learning.

I intend this book to be your go-to resource of literacy activities that make every minute in your classroom matter. I've compiled instructional ideas, routines, games, and activities to maximize every moment of the day. The book provides ample engaging, easy-to-prepare activities to infuse literacy throughout the day. Among the ideas will be wordplay, puzzles and riddles, and conversation starters all geared toward reading, writing, listening, and speaking.

As a reading researcher, I understand the importance of language and the power that words hold. Thus, I am deliberately rejecting the common lingo of "sponges" or "time fillers." *Sponge* implies that we are soaking up an excess of something; as teachers, we now face a shortage of time, not an excess. *Time fillers* implies that we are merely occupying time willy-nilly, with little purpose or intentional decision. As I've pointed out, our instructional time is too precious to simply fill. I've intentionally compiled activities that are *purposeful*. I include activities that further develop students as better speakers, listeners, writers, and readers.

Let me acknowledge that I am not always the original creator: I'd love to say that I created the brilliant Hink Pinks, but that is not true. Although I am not the original author of all of these ideas, this book is intended as a one-stop shopping compilation. So in addition to curating these ideas, I've done much of the vetting for you. Are you familiar with the term *dogfooding*? In her Cult of Pedagogy Podcast (a must-listen!), Jennifer Gonzalez defines dogfooding as "the act of using your own product as a consumer in order to work out its glitches, the metaphorical equivalent of eating your own dog food." Gonzalez suggests the following:

> Dogfood our lessons whenever possible. This means trying our own assignments. Taking our own tests. Doing our own homework. Attempting to actually complete those big projects. By doing this, we can detect all kind of problems that we'd never notice if we just created tasks and gave them straight to students.

During the year in which I wrote this book, I dogfooded these activities—either with children that I tutor, my own family members, or in classrooms where my friends teach.

THE #1 LITERACY ACTIVITY: INDEPENDENT READING

Before we dive into these activities, let me address my go-to literacy activity: independent reading. I firmly believe that students need and deserve daily independent reading in their classrooms—a belief that I wrote about in my 2018 International Literacy Association (ILA) position paper titled *The Power and Promise of Read-Alouds and Independent Reading*. Unfortunately, independent reading is not yet commonplace in classrooms today: a 2018 Scholastic survey highlighted that only 17% of students ages 6 to 17 reported daily in-school independent reading.

The benefits of independent reading are undeniable; the best readers are those who read the most, and the poorest readers are those who read the least. The more students read, the better their background knowledge, comprehension, fluency, vocabulary, self-efficacy as readers, and attitudes toward reading for pleasure. In-school independent reading fosters more frequent out-of-school reading (e.g., Miller & Moss, 2011; Stanovich, 1986). I particularly appreciate educator Kristin Ziemke's ideas about "sneaky reading," explained in *Game Changer! Book Access for All Kids* (Miller & Sharp, 2018):

> We sneak minutes with books as students turn in lunch money, unpack their bags and settle in for the day.... On the bus to field trips, waiting for lunch cleanup, and when our schedule unexpectedly changes, we read. (p. 99)

Though I adhere to the philosophy of "When in doubt, sit and read," independent reading cannot be our only activity. It's just not realistic for every student during every time of the day. Our teaching repertoire must be broader to address the wide variety of learners, contexts, and moments. Just as I foresee challenges in having second graders line up for the cafeteria while simultaneously independently reading, I also realize that sometimes our learners need more active ways to close out a lesson. Thus, I've consciously included the wide variety of activities that you will soon encounter.

Make Time for Independent Reading—Every Day!

If you're not already allowing time for your students to read independently in class, I recommend reading up on some of the research and strategies available to help you make independent reading a crucial (and beloved!) time for your students every day. Some great books about the benefits of independent reading, as well as effective ways to include it in the classroom routines and culture, include the following:

- Harvey, S., & Ward, A. (2017). *From striving to thriving: How to grow confident, capable readers.* New York, NY: Scholastic.

- Miller, D. (2009). *The book whisperer: Awakening the inner reader in every child.* San Francisco, CA: Jossey-Bass.

- Miller, D. (2013). *Reading in the wild: The book whisperer's keys to cultivating lifelong reading habits.* San Francisco, CA: Jossey-Bass.

- Miller, D., & Moss, B. (2011). *No more independent reading without support.* Portsmouth, NH: Heinemann.

- Miller, D., & Sharp, C. (2018). *Game changer! Book access for all kids.* New York, NY: Scholastic.

- Mulligan, T., & Landrigan, C. (2018). *It's all about the books: How to create bookrooms and classroom libraries that inspire readers.* Portsmouth, NH: Heinemann.

- Ripp, P. (2017). *Passionate readers: The art of reaching and engaging every child.* New York, NY: Routledge.

THE #1 LITERACY TOOL: READER'S NOTEBOOKS

Throughout this book, you will see references to activities that may be housed in students' Reader's Notebooks. A Reader's Notebook is a journal of reading-related activities that each student keeps over the course of the year. It is a place to grow ideas about books, to track reading behavior, to set and monitor reading goals, and to compile evidence of literacy-related behavior. I believe that every child—regardless of age, curriculum, or reading level—deserves a Reader's Notebook; I value Reader's Notebooks so much that I keep one myself. Though perhaps not the originators of Reader's Notebooks, Fountas and Pinnell (2018) explain the following:

> The notebook is a collection of thinking that reflects a student's reading life. It houses a variety of authentic responses to reading and the teacher's responses to thinking expressed by students. (p. 56)

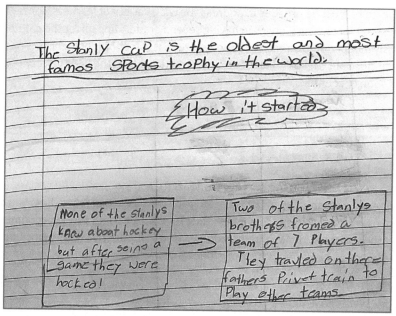

My fourth grader—an avid hockey player—used her Reader's Notebook to jot down key points from *What Is the Stanley Cup?* (Herman, 2019).

Keeping a Reader's Notebook helps children do the following:

- Envision themselves as readers
- Think about themselves in relation to books, including their interests, genres of preference, and reading habits
- Value reading and see reading as an invaluable part of their lives

The structure and format of Reader's Notebooks are a personal choice; a quick trip to Pinterest shows the variety of approaches. I keep mine simple by using a marble composition book for each year of my reading life. In any format, a Reader's Notebook should include the following elements:

- A large section for recording responses to reading
- A list of genres and a description of each
- Directions for giving book talks
- A place to record books to read or list books you love
- Tabs to indicate the different sections of the notebook

In addition, you'll find the appendix chock-full of resources. Reproducibles, game boards, and other essentials are housed in the appendix; you'll be directed there when needed. Also in the appendix is a handful of other goodies: (1) a compilation of quick activities (as not every activity needs a full-page explanation), (2) a suggested shopping list for some of my favorite classroom materials, and (3) a list of my favorite literacy-related board and card games. I've tried to be mindful that teachers have both limited time and limited budgets. Therefore, the activities in this book are mostly low cost and low prep. In a few instances, there are some commercial materials that you might need. Most of the materials can be purchased at a dollar store or a hardware store. If you don't have the necessary object, simply select another activity.

HOW TO USE THIS BOOK

Think of this book as a wander-around manual. It does not need to be followed in sequential order. Each page acts as a stand-alone guide. Its simplistic format enables you to apply the ideas immediately. This format ensures that you can easily flip to a double-page spread on a Tuesday afternoon when you've got an unexpected few extra moments, and use the experience in that moment. Peppered throughout the book are student examples to bring these activities to life.

For the most part, the advance preparation is minimal—although a handful of activities do require some materials (they are listed). The format for each double-page spread is as follows:

The book's appendix contains a number of additional suggestions, including a list of supplies that can be handy for a number of activities, a list of word-based games that I love, and a list of categories you can use for some of the activities. In addition, you'll find a number of downloadable blank printables in the online companion website—resources.corwin.com/everyminutematters—that you and your students can use in the activities. The online companion also contains suggestions for adjusting activities for distance learning and family play.

KEEP THE CONVERSATION GOING

In these pages, you will find my favorite activities, but by no means is this list complete. I am a firm believer in the power of professional learning opportunities afforded to us through technology and social media. To honor your ideas, continue the conversation, and showcase your brilliance, I've created a professional learning community on Facebook and Twitter that is fittingly named #everyminutematters. Do you have a trick of the trade that you frequently use? Share it with me and the #everyminutematters community. Post student work (with names removed or blacked out), snap photos of your kids (I like to replace student faces with an emoji to protect confidentiality), and let us know what you and your students are doing to make sure #everyminutematters.

Effective teachers use their time effectively. In an exploration of characteristics of effective teachers, Duke, Cervetti, and Wise (2018) note that their instructional routines were "characterized by a brisk pace of instruction and clear routines, thoroughly taught; participation structures; and engagement supports that maximized on-task behavior." This book will help you to meet that brisk pace of instruction so that our classrooms are places where students share our sense of urgency in maximizing the potential of every minute of our instructional day. As you move forward with this book and your teaching, I invite you to consider how you use your classroom instructional time. How do you explicitly or inferentially tell your students that your time together is precious? How do your instructional decisions and use of time showcase a sense of priority? How do you make every minute matter?

ACTiViTY WALKTHROUGH

Left-Hand Page

Link to Literacy: On each page you'll find an icon denoting the literacy focus of this activity: the ear signifies *listening*, the talking mouth represents *speaking*, the pencil represents *writing*, and the book indicates *reading*. In some cases, you'll see more than one icon as so many of these activities approach these foundational literacy skills holistically, rather than as separate.

Materials Needed: If any additional resources are needed, they will be explained here.

Quick Overview and Rationale: A brief explanation is given of the experience, any supporting research, and how the experience supports literacy.

Step-by-Step Directions: Written in a bulleted format for succinctness, this section will provide a step-by-step demonstration of how to replicate the experience in your classroom. Occasionally, these directions are broken into (1) teacher modeling and (2) student practice.

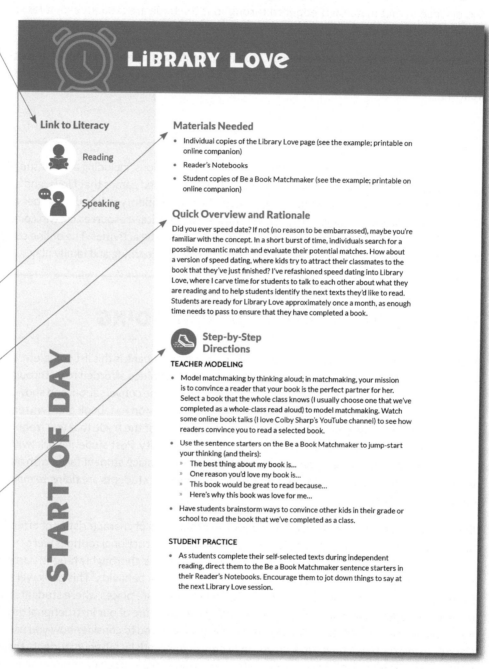

START OF DAY

LiBRARY LOve

Link to Literacy

Reading

Speaking

Materials Needed

- Individual copies of the Library Love page (see the example; printable on online companion)
- Reader's Notebooks
- Student copies of Be a Book Matchmaker (see the example; printable on online companion)

Quick Overview and Rationale

Did you ever speed date? If not (no reason to be embarrassed), maybe you're familiar with the concept. In a short burst of time, individuals search for a possible romantic match and evaluate their potential matches. How about a version of speed dating, where kids try to attract their classmates to the book that they've just finished? I've refashioned speed dating into Library Love, where I carve time for students to talk to each other about what they are reading and to help students identify the next texts they'd like to read. Students are ready for Library Love approximately once a month, as enough time needs to pass to ensure that they have completed a book.

Step-by-Step Directions

TEACHER MODELING

- Model matchmaking by thinking aloud; in matchmaking, your mission is to convince a reader that your book is the perfect partner for her. Select a book that the whole class knows (I usually choose one that we've completed as a whole-class read aloud) to model matchmaking. Watch some online book talks (I love Colby Sharp's YouTube channel) to see how readers convince you to read a selected book.

- Use the sentence starters on the Be a Book Matchmaker to jump-start your thinking (and theirs):
  » The best thing about my book is...
  » One reason you'd love my book is...
  » This book would be great to read because...
  » Here's why this book was love for me...

- Have students brainstorm ways to convince other kids in their grade or school to read the book that we've completed as a class.

STUDENT PRACTICE

- As students complete their self-selected texts during independent reading, direct them to the Be a Book Matchmaker sentence starters in their Reader's Notebooks. Encourage them to jot down things to say at the next Library Love session.

Moving Forward: This section includes possibilities to consider for quick, informal assessments and differentiation as well as extensions.

Minute Mentor: This brief section will include additional research and credits to the authors, creators, and researchers when relevant. If an experience is modified from other work or contributors, it will be acknowledged here.

- Break your students into two groups. I like to divide them into Peanut Butter and Jelly. (To help with management, I tell them that peanut butter is sticky and gooey, so Peanut Butters stay in their seat while Jellies move around.) Instruct students to find a partner (e.g., "Peanut Butters, stay in your seats, and Jellies, find a partner to sit next to or across from.").

- Give students short amounts of time to attract their partners to their books (I usually display 4 minutes on my SMART Board).

- After 2 to 3 minutes, give students a chance to make notes or record their thoughts on their Library Love handout.

- Rotate partners. Begin again, with the overarching goal being three to five rotations. I'd suggest each date be 3 minutes with four to six rotations.

- Encourage students to jot down the titles of the texts they'd most likely select in their Reader's Notebooks.

 Moving Forward

Find another classroom to mingle with. This encourages students to talk about their book selections across grade levels.

 Minute Mentor

This activity, while not new, is well outlined by literacy leaders Donalyn Miller and Colby Sharp. Check out Colby Sharp's blog (https://sharpread.wordpress.com), Donalyn Miller's books (*The Book Whisperer* [2009]; *Reading in the Wild* [2013]), and their collaborative text *Game Changer!: Book Access for All Kids* (2018).

Be a Book Matchmaker

Use these sentence starters to convince a classmate that she'd love your book!	
The best thing about my book is...	One reason you'd love my book is...
Here's why this book was love for me...	This book would be great to read because...

Edges of pages are color coordinated. Look for the...

- Pale blue edges for Start of Day

- Light blue edges for Transition Time

- Dark blue edges for Any Time

- Darkest blue edges for End of Day

PART ONE

Thinking Through Instructional Time

Songwriter Jim Croce—popular in the 1970s—once sang, "There never seems to be enough time to do the things we want to do once we find them." Maybe this sentiment echoes your feelings about instructional time in your classroom. When I provide professional learning in schools and districts, a common sentiment that I hear is this: "Sounds great. How do I find the time for this?" I usually try to push back—in a friendly, constructive manner—with the reminder that we find time for the things that we value. I try to adhere to his principle in my professional and personal life; when I remember that I value reading aloud to my young daughter or the healthy feeling that I get after a yoga class, I am more likely to step away from social media or turn off the television. The same is true for our classroom instruction. As you complete the detailed time audit (you will see this later in Part One), challenge yourself to connect your use of time to its associated value. Perhaps you'll find that Jim Croce's lyrics were not entirely accurate: there might be more time—than you originally thought—to do the things in your classroom that you want.

Before you flip ahead to the activities that will help you maximize your instructional time, reflect about how you're using your instructional time right now. In my work as a teacher educator, I often invite my graduate students to use time audits through their entire instructional day. I extend the same invitation to you now: Using a stopwatch for accountability, take some time to think through how every minute of your instructional day is used. Be sure to note transition times in these audits! How long do you spend on your morning meeting? Were you true to your intentions of spending 10 minutes in your word study instruction, or did it run long to 15 minutes? How long did it take your class to line up for lunch? Find a trusted colleague, and share your findings (or share them out in the Twitter community: #everyminutematters).

TiMe AUDiTS: WHY AND HOW

Time is a precious commodity. Bates and Morgan (2018) explain that "working within time constraints is best addressed intentionally and openly" (p. 132). As these authors explain, before we conduct time audits, we often underestimate how long instruction will take.

The purpose of a time audit is to examine how we use our instructional time with explicit focus on finding more time for instructional practices that have a direct impact on students' reading and writing. The end goal of a time audit is to engage in self-reflection and adjusting instruction as needed (Bates & Morgan, 2018). The following protocol is a modification from Bates and Morgan's 2018 article (a must-read about instructional time) and resources from the National Center on Time & Learning's Classroom Time Analysis Tool (CTAT). A time audit is relatively simple to do; you can do one on your own instruction or invite a trusted colleague to help you out.

> ## Managing the Logistics of a Time Audit
>
> Many of us are the only adult in a classroom, so here are a few tips on how to manage the logistics of a time audit. More extensive directions on how to do a time audit are provided later in this chapter:
>
> - Break the day into smaller chunks. For instance, start with a time audit of your English language arts block. It's more manageable to think through auditing the first half of a 90-minute block than an entire day. Set aside 5 to 10 days where you might audit 1 to 2 hours a day.

(Continued)

(Continued)

- Find a trusted colleague, and invite them in during their prep times. Be sure to return the favor. Be very clear that the purpose of their visit is to help you account for how time unfolds in your classroom.

- Think about additional personnel in your building who might have more flexibility in their schedules: literacy coaches, grade-level leaders, librarians or media specialists, parent volunteers, counselors, administrators, and so on. Invite them in for a short block of time with the clear purpose of helping you understand the breakdown of time in your classroom.

- Video yourself. Set up a tablet in the back of the classroom that will allow you to capture your instruction. Remember the focus is merely on how time is used, so don't overthink video and sound quality, camera angles, or other factors. You can then review it later with a stopwatch in hand.

The companion website contains two tracking sheets for a time audit. The Simple Time Audit is an open-ended chart (see a sample in Figure 1.1), whereas the Time Audit With Categories connects time to predetermined instructional routines (see Figure 1.2). You can download templates from the online companion, resources.corwin.com/everyminutematters.

FIGURE 1.1. SAMPLE OF A SIMPLE TIME AUDIT OF ENGLISH LANGUAGE ARTS BLOCK GRADE 1

Instructional Activity	Start Time	End Time	Total # of Minutes	Reflections
Start of Day (students enter, unpack, take seats)	8:40	8:53	13	Could this be streamlined? I was expecting this to be 10 minutes.
Welcome Students to Rug	8:53	8:56	3	This was quicker than I thought. What might I do here to make this more engaging?
Morning Meeting and Message (includes concepts of print in reading message, daily calendar)	8:56	9:13	17	I need to get this under 15 minutes to avoid squirmy students.
Whole-Class Phonics Instruction	9:14	9:29	15	Are there possibilities for differentiation?
Transition to Spelling Groups	9:30	9:32	2	The students knew exactly where to go!
Small-Group Word Study Instruction	9:33	9:55	22	This was a rotation of three groups from listening center, teacher-led group, and independent seatwork.
Transition to Carpet	10:02	10:06	4	This was a longer transition—probably due to putting materials away.
Whole-Class High-Frequency Word Instruction	10:07	10:12	5	We whizzed through these. Begin to look for transfer in student writing.

Instructional Activity	Start Time	End Time	Total # of Minutes	Reflections
Preview of Vocabulary Words	10:13	10:20	7	I was surprised by how many students seemed to recognize new words.
Read Aloud of *Brave Irene* With Think Alouds to Build Comprehension	10:21	10:40	19	I probably need to shorten this and incorporate more think-pair-shares for more frequent student discussion.
Guided Reading Groups (including rotation to listening centers and independent seatwork on writing)	10:41	11:24	43	Wow! I had no idea I spent so long on this!

FIGURE 1.2. SAMPLE OF A TIME AUDIT WITH CATEGORIES OF SECOND-GRADE ENGLISH LANGUAGE ARTS BLOCK

Categories of Time	Activities Within This Category	Start Time	End Time	Total Allotted Minutes
Teacher-Led Instruction	• Lesson introduction • Minilesson, lecture, read aloud, teacher modeling • Discussion or activity facilitated by teacher	9:13 10:46	9:56 11:23	43 minutes for phonics and word study instruction 37 minutes for reading or writing workshop
Student Work Time	• Small group discussion or activity • Independent practice or activity • Rotation through centers	8:20 9:56	9:03 10:03	43 minutes (morning seatwork) 7 minutes for phonics worksheet
Assessment of Student Learning	• Oral or written assessment of learning	9:56	10:30	7 minutes for phonics worksheet
Transition	• Arrival • Transitions within or outside of classroom • Dismissal • Unplanned interruption	9:04 10:31	9:12 10:45	8 minutes to transition to morning meeting 14 minutes to transition to snack and carpet

Follow these steps for a successful time audit:

- Select a portion of your literacy block that you'd like to audit. I suggest starting in 30- to 40-minute increments. It's helpful to plan a time audit as a recurring event; Bates and Morgan (2018) suggest auditing three different instructional days.

- On the tracking sheet of your choice, list the instructional practices. Feel free to shorten into manageable notes. For example, you might jot down "Read Aloud" to note that you spent

15 minutes conducting a whole-class interactive read aloud of *Miss Nelson Is Missing* while thinking aloud about inferencing.

- Be sure to identify transitional time and off-topic time. Using a stopwatch, record the beginning and ending time of each activity.

- Tally up your instruction so that you can compare your proposed teaching versus what actually occurred. For example, did you plan that your minilesson on metaphors would take 12 minutes but find it actually required 15 minutes? Use the final column to reflect on your findings.

- Continue your time audit across multiple days so that you might examine patterns and trends in your teaching.

- Engage in a reflective conversation about your instruction. This could be either an internal conversation, with your grade team, with a mentor teacher, or any trusted colleague. Think through these questions:

  » Did anything surprise you about your instructional time?

  » Where did you find yourself spending longer than anticipated? Where did you find yourself spending less time than planned?

  » Comment about the frequency of transitional time in your instruction. Were transitions smooth? Were your directions and expectations clear and reasonable? Was there any off-task behavior? How much time did it take for students to move from one thing to another?

  » Think through areas where you might be more efficient in your instruction. What instruction might be streamlined or reduced?

  » What instructional areas might deserve more time and attention? Where might you linger longer?

- As you scan to see the types of instructional activities that you provided, assess their importance to you and to your students. Reflect upon whether the allotted time matches its instructional importance. For instance, if you find yourself spending more time in your morning meeting than in a read aloud, does that use of time align to your instructional priorities?

Although I encourage you to begin this process as an individual, time audits can spark powerful, transformative shifts across school communities. Bates and Morgan (2018) encourage teachers to use time audits as follows:

- Begin school-based discussions about nonnegotiables in literacy instruction.

- Align instruction with its research base in order to prioritize best practices.

- Reduce or eliminate the practices that can be removed, to carve out more time for the nonnegotiables.

In my work as a teacher educator, I aspire to create reflective practitioners. Conducting time audits is a crucial step in reflection, as the process allows us a mirror into a classroom component over which we have some control: time. I began this chapter with the lyrics of a great 1970s musician, so let me add another in here—this time from an arguably more recognizable band: the Rolling Stones. In their 1964 Billboard chart hit, they sang, "Time is on my side." Perhaps after conducting a thoughtful audit of your instruction, you, too, will find that time is on your side.

MAXIMIZE YOUR ROUTINES AND TRANSITION TIMES

To write this book, I spent time in K–5 classrooms to get a sense of usual classroom routines and how the day unfolds. Through these observations, I noted four times during the school day ripe with opportunity. I'll run through these four times quickly here, and then I'll dig a bit deeper into each.

1. *First thing in the day, often known as morning meeting, "do now," or seatwork:* I refer to these activities as **Start of Day.** You can quickly reference these with the palest blue page edges.

2. *The myriad transitional times, when students leave and enter the classroom from specials such as lunch, recess, gym, music, library, and art; move within the classroom to various activities; or line up to leave the classroom:* I group these activities to be used in **Transition Time.** You'll find these with the light blue page edges.

3. *Those oddball minutes that unexpectedly arise in the day, when lessons run short, you're waiting to be called into the auditorium for class photos, or technology fails and disrupts your carefully planned lesson:* I refer to these activities as **Any Time.** These can be located with the dark blue page edges.

4. *The end of the day, when you are simultaneously exhausted and frantic to bring closure to new learning:* These closure activities are essential in extending learning, checking for understanding, and transferring learning to new situations. I refer to these as **End of Day,** found with the darkest blue page edges.

Start of Day

The beginning of the day is crazy time in the classroom! We are juggling our coffee cups, attendance sheets, homework folders, notes from parents, daily schedule changes, and on and on. Sometimes kids are eager to see us, bursting with updates and conversation. Other times, kids drag in, shouldering untold challenges from their home lives. As we greet children and get a sense of students' moods, we remind students (even in February) that their backpacks and coats go in cubbies, and homework packets go in the appropriate bin. In my classroom observations, I've noticed that the most prevalent starts to the day are (1) the ever-popular morning meeting and (2) the ever-present seatwork (or "do now"). Let's dig a bit deeper into each of these practices to understand their intent and how they sometimes go astray.

The Morning Meeting

Intended to be a community-building classroom routine, the morning meeting allots time for students to greet each other, engage in oral language activities, review the day ahead, and build social skills. While all of these components are essential, we must be careful not to fall into the trap of the "marathon morning meeting" (Brinkerhoff & Roehrig, 2014, p. 55). Are you using up precious moments because one student goes on and on about a story he wanted to tell? Are you still doing the calendar, weather, and days of the week in fourth grade?

The morning meeting should last 10 to 15 minutes, and it should build the momentum and energy for the day (rather than drone on wearily). If your morning meeting is becoming a marathon, I encourage you to heed the advice of Brinkerhoff and Roehrig (2014), who remind us that "each activity should be carefully analyzed and monitored to ensure that it is worthy of the time spent" (p. 55). Perhaps as you discover some of the ideas and experiences in this book, you'll be motivated to shorten that marathon meeting.

Seatwork

For so many students, seatwork is a ubiquitous part of their morning. After filtering into classrooms, putting away belongings, turning in homework, sharpening pencils, taking chairs off tables, and doing all those other housekeeping tasks, they sit quietly in their desks and set to work on a "do now." Most of the time, this morning seatwork is a packet of worksheets, assigned workbook pages, or problems written on the board.

No doubt this typical morning routine calms the initial frenzy following the morning bell, but it too often leaves students feeling anxious, rushed, and disengaged. Furthermore, many of these morning work rituals offer little instructional value. I think back (with a silent cringe) to my first years in the classroom; my students would copy down an intentionally created grammatically incorrect sentence from the whiteboard and then correct the errors. My attempt to teach grammar was mind-blowingly boring, decontextualized from authentic literacy, and did nothing to improve their understanding of when to use a semicolon in their own writing.

In the midst of the hustle and bustle, we must be mindful that our first 15 minutes of the day should be welcoming and purposeful. The ideal start to the day achieves the following:

- Makes students feel seen and welcomed
- Provides a smooth, efficient transition from outside of school to formal learning environment
- Focuses students for a meaningful day of learning
- Honors student choice about the structures and activities that work best for them

The Start of Day activities are literacy-rich ideas that offer choice and independence first thing in the morning. Their intent is to get the instructional day going in a way that engages students, sets the appropriate tone for the day, and honors authentic literacy.

Transition Time

Does your classroom feel like a frenzy—students pulled out for interventions, a parade of traffic from band practice and choir rehearsal, kids coming and going from specials, bathroom trips, and errands? It can be maddening to find a time in elementary classrooms without these inevitable transitions, which occur both outside of and within classrooms. Kids move in and out of the classroom for lunch, PE, art, library, music, and recess. Even within the classroom, kids are often on the move. They transition from one content focus to another, to centers, and from activity to activity. These transition times are crucial; a well-planned transition time minimizes disruption and inattention, whereas a chaotic transition gobbles up precious time and may lead to issues in classroom management.

Let's think back to that study (Ness, 2011, 2016) that I mentioned in the introduction. In 3,000 minutes of classroom observation, I witnessed 285 minutes of transition. That equaled 12% of lost instructional time. What a missed opportunity for creative, engaging, literacy-based ways to make the most of that transition time. Don't believe me? Consider the wisdom of Wiley Blevins, expert on early reading. In his 2017 book, Blevins wrote the following:

> Instructional time is valuable, and time lost in transitioning from one activity to another is time you can't get back. I have observed teachers losing 10–15 minutes of

instructional time distributing [materials]. This adds up quickly. In one week, it can be over an hour of instructional time lost. We can't let this happen. (p. 223)

These transitions are inevitable yet need not be lost times. Ideally, transition times unfold as follows:

- Direct students on how to best prepare for upcoming activities
- Minimize disruption while maximizing focus and attention
- Keep students engaged while optimizing learning

Let's take a peek into an exemplary classroom—that of Mr. Allen, whom my daughter had as her third-grade teacher. I visited the classroom one day in November, to serve as a parent volunteer for whatever that particular week's project was. Upon my arrival, the students were out of the classroom; I had arrived early and waited for them to return from lunch and recess. As they filed in, I was flabbergasted by the efficiency with which they returned and settled back into their instructional routine. The frenzy of replacing empty lunch boxes into cubbies, hanging up jackets and sweatshirts, washing grimy hands, making visits to the water fountain, scraping chairs out from underneath desks, and rehashing of four-square victories lasted less than 3 minutes. Mr. Allen barely said a word; students knew exactly what to do in this transitional time.

On the board, Mr. Allen had written these directions:

Choose one, and jot your answer in your Reader's Notebook:

Would you rather …

- Be really fast or really strong?
- Be the worst player on a team that always wins OR be the best player on a team that always loses?
- Always have a cough or always be itchy?

I watched students silently read directions written on the whiteboard and crack open their Reader's Notebooks. A handful of students sketched in their journals; when I inquired about this, Mr. Allen explained that these students were English language learners, and sketching was afforded differentiation to jump-start their writing. All students were engaged in their writing and able to select a choice that motivated them. Even better, they were building the seeds for persuasive writing—without knowing it! With this Would You Rather? exercise (directions provided later on), Mr. Allen made the most of that pesky transitional time. No doubt Mr. Allen was a master of classroom management. Students in his classroom had internalized the message about the importance of classroom time. For a brief second, I thought back to my early teaching experiences and ruminated on the time I had lost during similar transitional times. The activities identified as Transition Time help us to reclaim the inevitable transitions and repurpose them with literacy-rich activities—perhaps even smoothing some classroom management challenges.

Any Time

What teacher hasn't had the experience of "Oops! That didn't take as long as I thought it would." Though instructional time is short, there are also moments when there's too much time and we scramble for meaningful ways to use that time. For me, these were the moments when a lesson ended and there was not enough time to embark on something new. These were the times when I was waiting for the photographer to call my students into the auditorium for the class photo, when I was battling a cold and silently willing the final bell to ring, and the brutal stretch before holiday vacations. Maybe we don't have the time, energy, patience, or materials needed to launch into something new, and the time is short enough that telling kids to take out a book for independent reading would be a tease. Now, with the activities in this book, you have options for literacy-rich activities that support instructional goals more than word hunts or crossword puzzles.

I used to call these sponge activities, with the idea of soaking up extra class time as a sponge soaks up kitchen counter spills. As I understand more and more about the importance of word choice, I've steered away from the word *sponge*, as it seems to imply that these activities exist solely to occupy time. On the contrary, these activities make the most of those hidden or unexpected moments of classroom time: when lessons run short, students finish early, or we find other unexpected bonus minutes in the classroom.

End of Day

If you were to visit my classroom in my rookie teaching year, you'd shake your head at the lost instructional time. In those final minutes before the bell, I'd likely be imploring, "Don't pack up yet! The bell hasn't rung!" The desks would be out of their original rows, there would be garbage on the floor, and my students might be whispering to each other, "Did she assign homework yet?" As I'd be directing one cluster of students to straighten up their tables, I'd be hurrying another handful of students to turn in the assignments that they had not yet completed. As a result, the end of the day felt frenetic and disorganized.

Let me explain the routine that ends every yoga class I've ever attended in my 20 years of being a practicing yogi. The last 5 to 10 minutes are typically called *savasana*, or an extended rest and relaxation time. This is a time of utter silence, where you lay in stillness (known as the corpse pose). This element—meant to seal the practice—serves to invigorate us after hard work in this session, release stress, improve physical and emotional well-being, and leave us eagerly anticipating the next session. Admittedly, it's my favorite time of each yoga session, and when I've had to dash out of a yoga session early, I sorely miss reaping the benefits of the final routine.

What if the end of our instructional day followed a similar approach? I'm not suggesting that we encourage our students to lie on the floor in absolute silence and stillness (though this might certainly appeal to exhausted teachers!). Instead, let's explore the possibilities that arise when we set instructional routines that wrap up learning, set a course for the rest of the week, and send students home invigorated and yearning for tomorrow's lesson. In fact, research indicates that closure activities help students digest, retain, and assimilate new learning:

> Students need closure to help them give their learning lasting relevance for their lives, to reflect, to solidify and internalize what they've learned [e.g., Lia, 2014; Pollock, 2007; Wolf & Supon, 1994]. This requires more than statements by teachers of what has been learned and why; students need to be actively involved, as Cavanaugh et al. [1996] concluded. (Ganske, 2017, p. 99)

The end of the day should be a combination of both backward and forward thinking: *backward thinking* for students to synthesize their daily learning and *forward thinking* for students to anticipation the next direction in their learning. The activities suggested as End of Day give a quick review of lessons, provide closure and follow-up, and paint an overview of the next steps in their future learning. When students leave the classroom confident that their time is precious, they are eager to return for more learning the next day.

THiNK FLeXiBLY

Now that you've got a clear sense of how to use this book, when to incorporate these literacy-rich activities, and why to time audit your own instruction, you've got the green light to peruse the activities. Here is a final note before you start: I encourage you to think flexibly. By this, I mean that the classification and organization of these activities are suggestions, not a strict format. There are some activities that lend themselves logically to particular times of the day: For instance, Lining Up With Literacy is ideal for the transitional time when children line up to leave the classroom. But just because I suggest that Rotate Your Writing is a Start of Day activity does not mean that you can't modify it to use as an End of Day activity. Also keep in mind that the literacy icons on each page are suggestions and that literacy is a rich and multifaceted entity in which the skills of reading, writing, listening, and thinking are richly intertwined. As you examine each activity, you'll see the icons depicting which literacy skill is the closest fit, but many of these activities involve more than one component.

As you think flexibly and tweak and adjust each activity to meet the diverse needs of the learners in your environment, I encourage you to share them with the Every Minute Matters communities on social media by using #everyminutematters. Not only will you grow your professional learning network but you'll gain new ideas to transform your classroom into a literacy-rich environment in which every minute matters toward sustained student learning, deeper engagement, and—dare I say it—fun.

PART TWO

Literacy-Rich Experiences at Your Fingertips

Remember to think flexibly as you page through the activities on the pages that follow. Although they are organized (loosely) around what type of transitional time they work best in, I decided not to put strict rules on organization because you might decide to use any of these activities in any time of day or type of transition based on in-the-moment need of your students and your instructional time. So, you'll notice there are activities designated *Start of Day, Transition Time, Any Time,* and *End of Day*—but just because the activity is labeled *Start of Day* doesn't mean you can't use it before the end-of-day dismissal bell.

You'll also notice icons throughout the activities, which designate *reading, writing, listening,* and *speaking.* These icons are intended to give you an at-a-glance sense of the literacy skill the activity reinforces. Sometimes there are multiple icons because an activity supports multiple skills.

Reading

Writing

Listening

Speaking

I decided, too, not to organize these activities around age or grade level because, frankly, children vary so much! I trust you'll be able to determine which activities your students will enjoy, which they are ready to attempt, and which might have to wait until later in the year after they've had more foundational instruction in an area.

Refer to the Activity Walkthrough chart in the front of the book for a clearer look across all activities so you can flip right to the one you need when you need it. That chart also lists more specific subskills that each activity enhances.

I hope you'll use these activities whenever you need them, adapt them, and share more with me and the #everyminutematters community. Most of all, I hope your students have fun applying their literacy skills in meaningful new ways throughout the day.

ROTATE YOUR WRITING

START OF DAY

Link to Literacy

 Writing

Materials Needed

- Age-appropriate writing paper, or writing journals
- Online timer to help countdown time (I like using the Google timer on my SMART Board.)

Quick Overview and Rationale

Wouldn't it be awesome if kids approached writing with excitement? What if writing became collaborative, enjoyable, and gave students immediate audiences? All of this is possible with kids with Rotate Your Writing.

Step-by-Step Directions

TEACHER MODELING

- Using a document camera or large sticky note, think aloud as you add to prestarted writing. For instance, you might take two sheets of paper, one starting with "Once upon a time" and the other with "You'll never believe what happened." On one page, you might talk through or write out how you'd continue the writing that you received, highlighting that you are not aiming to finish the story but just to continue it. On the other page, you might call on students to brainstorm ideas of how they'd add to the writing that they received.

STUDENT PRACTICE

- Each student begins with a blank piece of paper (or their writing journals) and has 3 to 5 minutes to start a story. Students can begin in whatever way they'd like. Some students will benefit from story starters like the ones listed in online story starter resources. Try some from the following online resources!
  - » http://www.scholastic.com/teachers/story-starters
  - » https://www.literacyshed.com/story-starters.html
  - » https://www.journalbuddies.com/creative-writing-2/creative-writing-story-starters
  - » https://www.creative-writing-now.com/story-starters.html
- After the allotted time (3 to 5 minutes), have students pass their papers to another student. Each student reads the paper they've received and then writes on that same paper, picking up where the original author left off. Allow students to write for the same amount of time in the second round.

- You may provide as many rounds as needed for your students. Ideally, each paper should have contributions from at least four classmates.
- The paper should be returned to the original author, and give students time to read their classmates' additions.

Moving Forward

Follow up this activity with conversations about how students' writing changed and evolved as it rotated. You might use conversation starters like these:

- When you began your writing, what idea did you have in your mind for how it would end?
- Tell me about how your writing changed as other people added to it.
- What surprised you about your story and how others added to it?
- What would you say to the other authors, who added to your writing?
- When you got a new piece of writing, what strategies and thinking did you use to add to it?

Minute Mentor

Have you heard of Consequences or Exquisite Corpse? If not, check them out with a quick Google search. These old parlor games from the 1910s emerged as artists wrote on a sheet of paper, folded it to conceal their writing, and passed it to the next contributor. Rotate Your Writing plays off of these, with the primary difference that children can read the full story before adding to it (as opposed to the line above).

READER'S NOTEBOOK TOURS

START OF DAY

Link to Literacy

 Reading

Materials Needed

- Reader's Notebooks
- Sticky notes

Quick Overview and Rationale

Too often, we lose the power of Reader's Notebooks by keeping them a solitary pursuit. When readers showcase their notebooks, they embrace literacy as a social activity and engage in rich conversations around reading. I find that every 4 to 6 weeks is the ideal time to tour Reader's Notebooks.

 ## Step-by-Step Directions

TEACHER MODELING

- Explain that one way to grow as a community of readers is to invite other people to explore their Reader's Notebooks.

- Using a document camera, model a few pages of your Reader's Notebook. Think aloud as you talk through a few pages that you'd want to share with fellow readers and what they reveal about you as a reader.

- Tell students that if they don't want anyone to see a particular page in their notebook that they can fold it in half.

- Provide anchor charts with the following prompts, or display them in an easily visible place.
  » The most interesting thing in my Reader's Notebook is...
  » I am proudest of this part of my notebook because...
  » Here's what my notebook shows about my reading and learning...

STUDENT PRACTICE

- Use sticky notes to mark a handful of pages to showcase to students

- Share out these pages, and use the following sentence starters to explain why you've selected these pages.
  » The most interesting thing in my Reader's Notebook is...
  » I am proudest of this part of my notebook because...
  » Here's what my notebook shows about my reading and learning...

- Set a timer (3–5 minutes) for students to walk through their own notebooks and use sticky notes to flag the pages that they want to share.

Have students share their notebooks in partners, using language from above to scaffold their conversations.

Moving Forward

To encourage students to be metacognitive about themselves as readers, turn these conversations into writing. You might have them do periodic writing where they explore what their notebooks reveal about their development as readers. To jump-start their writing, students might begin with these prompts:

- When I look through my notebook, I see…
- My Reader's Notebook shows _____ about my reading.

Minute Mentor

For additional information about Reader's Notebooks, check out the following resources:

- https://www.scholastic.com/teachers/blog-posts/beth-newingham/readers-notebook
- https://choiceliteracy.com/article/strategies-for-using-readers-notebooks

I am reading Frindle by Andrew Clements. Nick wants to use the word Frindle but MS. Ganger is getting in the way. MS. Ganger is getting in the way because she wants to stop it. She is also in the way because she is making kids stay after school.

Great! You are growing the idea about Nick's biggest obstacle — Mrs. Granger! Keep collecting evidence that she is getting in his way!

A glimpse into a third grader's Reader's Notebook, along with a quick written response from her teacher.

Notes

LIBRARY LOVE

Link to Literacy

Reading

Speaking

Materials Needed

- Individual copies of the Library Love page (see the example; printable on online companion)

- Reader's Notebooks

- Student copies of Be a Book Matchmaker (see the example; printable on online companion)

Quick Overview and Rationale

Did you ever speed date? If not (no reason to be embarrassed), maybe you're familiar with the concept. In a short burst of time, individuals search for a possible romantic match and evaluate their potential matches. How about a version of speed dating, where kids try to attract their classmates to the book that they've just finished? I've refashioned speed dating into Library Love, where I carve time for students to talk to each other about what they are reading and to help students identify the next texts they'd like to read. Students are ready for Library Love approximately once a month, as enough time needs to pass to ensure that they have completed a book.

 ## Step-by-Step Directions

TEACHER MODELING

- Model matchmaking by thinking aloud; in matchmaking, your mission is to convince a reader that your book is the perfect partner for her. Select a book that the whole class knows (I usually choose one that we've completed as a whole-class read aloud) to model matchmaking. Watch some online book talks (I love Colby Sharp's YouTube channel) to see how readers convince you to read a selected book.

- Use the sentence starters on the Be a Book Matchmaker to jump-start your thinking (and theirs):
    » The best thing about my book is...
    » One reason you'd love my book is...
    » This book would be great to read because...
    » Here's why this book was love for me...

- Have students brainstorm ways to convince other kids in their grade or school to read the book that we've completed as a class.

STUDENT PRACTICE

- As students complete their self-selected texts during independent reading, direct them to the Be a Book Matchmaker sentence starters in their Reader's Notebooks. Encourage them to jot down things to say at the next Library Love session.

- Break your students into two groups. I like to divide them into Peanut Butter and Jelly. (To help with management, I tell them that peanut butter is sticky and gooey, so Peanut Butters stay in their seat while Jellies move around.) Instruct students to find a partner (e.g., "Peanut Butters, stay in your seats, and Jellies, find a partner to sit next to or across from.").

- Give students short amounts of time to attract their partners to their books (I usually display 4 minutes on my SMART Board).

- After 2 to 3 minutes, give students a chance to make notes or record their thoughts on their Library Love handout.

- Rotate partners. Begin again, with the overarching goal being three to five rotations. I'd suggest each date be 3 minutes with four to six rotations.

- Encourage students to jot down the titles of the texts they'd most likely select in their Reader's Notebooks.

 **Moving Forward**

Find another classroom to mingle with. This encourages students to talk about their book selections across grade levels.

 **Minute Mentor**

This activity, while not new, is well outlined by literacy leaders Donalyn Miller and Colby Sharp. Check out Colby Sharp's blog (https://sharpread.wordpress.com), Donalyn Miller's books (*The Book Whisperer* [2009]; *Reading in the Wild* [2013]), and their collaborative text *Game Changer!: Book Access for All Kids* (2018).

Be a Book Matchmaker

Use these sentence starters to convince a classmate that she'd love your book!	
The best thing about my book is...	One reason you'd love my book is...
Here's why this book was love for me...	This book would be great to read because...

Library Love Ranking Sheet

1. I think I'm in LOVE.

2. Intriguing, let's spend some more time together

3. Maybe...

4. Not my type

Book #1

Book #2

Book #3

Book #4

The Book With No Pictures

Be a Book Matchmaker

Use these sentence starters to convince a classmate that s/he'd love your book!

The best thing about my book...	One reason you'd love my book is...
is that it is funny.	because it makes you laugh.
Here's why this book was love for me...	This book would be great to read because...
because when I'm sad it makes me laugh.	it has so many funny words.

This third grader convinces a classmate that the popular B. J. Novak's *The Book With No Pictures* is a worthwhile read.

"I WONDER" WRITING

Link to Literacy

 Writing

Materials Needed

- Student writing journals, or age-appropriate writing paper
- Curiosity-provoking props (see explanation in directions)
- Anchor charts with question-generation language

Quick Overview and Rationale

Kids are naturally curious. A survey of 1,000 mothers showed that children ages 4 to 10 ask an average of 288 questions a day (Telegraph Staff, 2013). "I Wonder" Writing aims to harness the power of student-generated questions, as questioning motivates students, creates engaged and purposeful readers, and increases memory (see Ness, 2015). In my work around student-generated questions, I invest in a weekly time for questioning; I often use children's questions as a way to connect nonfiction text to their innate curiosity. For instance, a first grader's question of "If there is a Big Dipper and a Little Dipper, why is there no Medium Dipper?" led us to investigate the answer with books on constellations.

 **Step-by-Step Directions**

TEACHER MODELING

- Model some teacher-generated questions, and discuss why you asked this question. Here are some examples:
  - » As I walked to school, I found this piece of an eggshell, which I think came from a bird. It made me wonder all sorts of questions that I can write for my I Wonder writing. I wonder what kind of bird this egg came from? What are eggshells made of? What happened to the baby inside this egg? Can you help me think of some other questions that I might ask?

- On anchor charts, display question-generation academic language, such as these:
  - » I wonder….
  - » Who?
  - » What?
  - » Where?
  - » When?
  - » Why?
  - » How?

STUDENT PRACTICE

In 5 to 10 minutes, allow students to generate a list of their questions. Younger students might draw an illustration of their questions.

Return to the process of questioning to jump-start conversations about content instruction. For example, you might say, "Today we're going to start our unit on weather. What do you wonder about weather?"

Questions beget questions, but some students might need a jump start. Props or photos work well to springboard questions. You might bring in an object from the natural world (a shell, a rock, a pine cone) or picture on your SMART Board. In a first-grade classroom, I displayed a picture of a construction site that was around the corner from the school. The picture showed mounds of rock and dirt, heavy machinery, and an enormous pit in the ground. Students were practically jumping out of their seats to share their questions!

Moving Forward

- Students who need additional writing support will benefit from sentence starters, in which they complete prompts like "I wonder..." or "A question that I have is..."

Minute Mentor

For more information on "I Wonder" Writing, check out Harvey Daniels's (2017) *The Curious Classroom: 10 Structures for Teaching with Student-Directed Inquiry*. Or check out these articles:

- Distefano, D. & Ness, M. (2018). Using hand symbols to scaffold student-generated questions in kindergarten classrooms. *Young Children, 73*, 22–28.

- Ness, M. (2015). *The question is the answer: Supporting student-generated queries in elementary classrooms.* Landover, MD: Rowman & Littlefield.

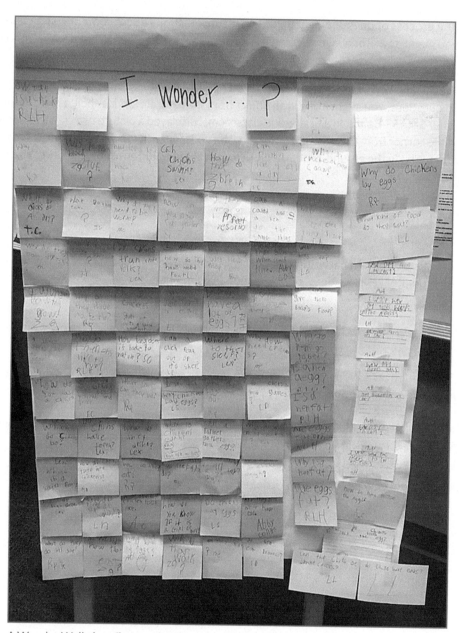

A Wonder Wall gives first graders lots of room to jot their questions.

A first grader writes down her daily wondering.

BEACH BALL BONANZA

Link to Literacy

 Listening

 Speaking

START OF DAY

Materials Needed

- A permanent marker
- An inflatable beach ball (available at most toy stores or dollar stores)

Quick Overview and Rationale

I'm all for getting kids up and active, especially when it involves learning! In the early days of my teaching career, I tossed a beach ball through my classroom to do exactly that. Each colored panel of the beach ball had a different prompt on it. All sorts of "learning balls" are available from commercial retailers; save yourself the $15, and make one yourself!

 Step-by-Step Directions

TEACHER MODELING

- Using a permanent marker, write open-ended prompts on each section of the beach ball. Ideas include the following:
  » Sight words: Students read the sight word and use it in a sentence.
  » Comprehension questions: "Give your favorite part of the book" or "Here's why I'd recommend the book to a friend."
  » Vocabulary: While throwing the ball, the teacher shouts out a vocabulary word. The panels might read "Use it in a sentence," "Give a synonym," etc.

- Have a child softly toss the ball to you, carefully pointing out "I like how you threw it gently underhand, toward my open hands" (reinforce that this isn't dodgeball!).

- Model the process of following the prompts written on the ball. For instance, you might say, "I'm picking up my right thumb to read what it says. My thumb landed on the section 'Use the word in a sentence.' The vocabulary word is *furious*, so my sentence might be 'I felt furious when my brother broke my favorite toy.'"

STUDENT PRACTICE

- When kids catch the ball, they read the prompt underneath their right thumb and share their answer before tossing the ball to a classmate.

Moving Forward

There are endless possibilities to incorporate this across the curriculum. At the beginning of the year, I use the beach ball to build classroom community (e.g., "Tell us your name and your favorite thing to do after school"). Studying geography? Use a dry erase marker to write states on the panels, and students provide the capital. Beach Ball Bonanza is also fun to wrap up the end of the day (e.g., "Tell us some kind behavior that you saw in school today," "The most interesting part of the day was...").

Minute Mentor

Check out the body of research on movement and learning. In fact, the Centers for Disease Control and Prevention explains that classroom physical activity benefits students by doing the following:

- Improving their concentration and ability to stay on task in the classroom
- Reducing disruptive behavior, such as fidgeting, in the classroom
- Improving their motivation and engagement in the learning process
- Helping to improve their academic performance (higher grades and test scores)
- Increasing their amount of daily physical activity

Here's another quick read:

- https://www.edweek.org/tm/articles/2017/08/08/learning-in-motion-bring-movement-back-to.html

LAUGHING THROUGH REREADINGS

Link to Literacy

 Reading

 Speaking

Materials Needed

- Kid-appropriate joke books, or websites with jokes. Here are some of my favorite websites and authors:
  » https://www.ducksters.com/jokes
  » https://funkidsjokes.com
  » https://www.rd.com/jokes/kids

- Brewer, P. (2003). *You must be joking!: Cool jokes, plus 17 ½ tips for remembering, telling, and making up your own jokes.* Battle Creek, MI: Cricket.

- Dahl, M. (2002). *The everything kids' joke book: Side-splitting, rib-tickling fun!* Cincinnati, OH: Adams Media.

- Horsfall, J. (2003). *Kids' silliest jokes.* New York, NY: Sterling.

- Terban, M. (2007). *Eight ate: A feast of homonym riddles.* New York, NY: Sandpiper.

- Weitzman, I. (2006). *Jokelopedia: The biggest, best, silliest, dumbest joke book ever.* New York, NY: Workman.

Quick Overview and Rationale

Fluency practice too often focuses on speed and accuracy and overlooks the role of prosody and intonation! Fluent readers are pleasant to listen to, as they know what words to emphasize, when to pause, and how to vary their inflection and tone. Jokes are the quintessential texts for oral delivery; they require that a reader attend to punctuation, intonation, and phrasing. Certainly, everyone has listened to a poor joke delivery and thought, "The joke was funny, but the delivery was lousy!" A joke teller who isn't fluid in delivery, who pauses too long or not long enough, or who doesn't emphasize the right words will not get the desired reaction. No doubt there is a link to comprehension here as well, as the joke teller has to understand the words and their interaction in order to emphasize accurately—and the way they deliver affects the listener's comprehension, too. Motivate your students to improve their oral delivery as they laugh through rereadings!

 ## Step-by-Step Directions

TEACHER MODELING

- Lead a whole-class conversation in what makes a good joke teller. You might show quick videos of kid-friendly comedians to evoke conversations about phrasing, pauses, and word stress.

- Model ineffective and effective joke telling, and collect feedback on how you could improve your delivery. The example below might jump-start your modeling:

> » *Doctor, Doctor, I feel like a strawberry. Well, it sounds like you're in a real jam.* (e.g., What do I need to do to my voice and delivery to make this joke as funny as possible? Yes, I need to stress the word *jam* since the humor is in the wordplay of the double meaning of *jam*.)

- Examine other jokes to point out punctuation, including question marks, commas, periods, and exclamation marks, and discuss what purpose they hold in the joke's meaning and humor. Explain how the punctuation affects the reader's voice, word emphasis, timing, and expression.

STUDENT PRACTICE

- Have students work with partners to tell or reread jokes. Partners should listen and evaluate each other for their expression, timing, and delivery.

- Continue to laugh through fluency practice as students aim to improve their joke delivery.

Moving Forward

- You might have students use the recording feature on classroom tablets to make short videos of themselves delivering jokes. They can watch themselves (and/or their classmates) to evaluate their performance and aim to improve their delivery.

- Give students time over several days to practice their jokes in preparation for "Comedy Hour," a time when students perform their jokes as comedians for classroom visitors.

Minute Mentor

Read more here:

- Ness, M. (2009). Laughing through rereadings: Using joke books to build fluency. *The Reading Teacher, 62,* 691–694.

For more information on prosody, fluency, and instructional ideas, check out the work of Timothy Rasinksi. I'm particularly fond of this one:

- Rasinski, T., & Smith, M. C. (2018). *The megabook of fluency.* New York, NY: Scholastic.

READ, RECORD, REFLECT

Link to Literacy

Listening

Speaking

Materials Needed

- iPads or other tablets, which allow students to make quick videos of themselves reading

- Short passages for fluency practice (written at students' independent or instructional levels)

- Anchor charts that show how to note fluency errors:
  - » When they omit a word
  - » When they substitute a word
  - » When they invert the order of words
  - » When they insert a word that is not in the text

- Student copies of the Read, Record, Reflect checklist (download available from the online companion website: resources.corwin.com/everyminutematters)

Quick Overview and Rationale

Need a 21st-century upgrade for your fluency instruction? Incorporate iPads' easy video recording capacities. In a simple process of Read, Record, Reflect, students have opportunities to hear their own oral reading and become aware of their own prosody, expression, and intonation.

 ## Step-by-Step Directions

TEACHER MODELING

- Take a video of yourself reading aloud, modeling how you record yourself.

- Demonstrate how to tap the camera icon to start recording, and then tap the record button again to stop recording.

- As you read a short passage, intentionally make some errors so that you can later demonstrate how to mark your errors.

- Lead the whole class in watching the video to correct your errors; display a copy of the text, and showcase how to mark errors.

- For omissions, use a strike-through.

- For substitutions, write the incorrect word above the correct word.

- For inversions, draw an arrow to indicate incorrect sequencing.

- For insertions, add a caret with the inserted word.

- Use the time stamp on the video to lead students in a reflection with the Read, Record, Reflect checklist.

STUDENT PRACTICE

- Match students with short passages written at their independent or instructional levels so that students can read with minimal assistance.

- Have them watch their videos as they mark their errors (I like to put copies into plastic sleeves so that students can mark up their errors with a dry erase pen and then wipe them clean when finished).

- Encourage students to re-create their videos until they've reduced their errors and increased their prosody.

- When they are satisfied with their videos, students can complete the Read, Record, Reflect checklist.

 **Moving Forward**

- Have students work in pairs to evaluate each other's videos. You might provide sentence starters to help them with the language, including the following:
    - » I noticed…
    - » The best thing that my partner's video showed was…
    - » One thing my partner could improve is…

- Create a private class channel (or YouTube channel) where students uploaded their clips. This video library can be shared with parents and families. Parents can comment on videos directly underneath each video.

- If your class has a "reading buddy partnership," students might share their videos with their buddies from other classrooms or grade levels.

 **Minute Mentor**

Read more in my article:

- Ness, M. (2017). "Is that what I really sound like?": Using iPads for fluency practice. *The Reading Teacher*, 70, 611–615. doi:10.1002/trtr.1554

Read-Record-Reflect Checklist

_____'s Fluency Reflection

Title: _____

Listen to your recording and your fluency using this rubric.

Iˢᵗ Reading   How long did it take you?_____ Date _____

		☺	☆
I read with EXPRESSION. (Not like a robot.)	✓	☺	☆
I read in PHRASES. (Pausing at punctuation marks.)	✓	☺	☆
My RATE was just right. (Not too fast, not too slow.)	✓	☺	☆
I read the words ACCURATELY.	✓	☺	☆

I will work on _____.

Notes

BOOK TASTING

Link to Literacy

 Reading

Materials Needed

- Stacks of books of various reading levels and genre. I typically aim for three to five books per child.

- If you're a Pinterest-worthy teacher (not at all me!), it's engaging to create a restaurant vibe in your classroom, with tablecloths, place mats, battery-operated candles, vases of fake flowers, and so on.

- One copy of the Book Tasting Menu per child (download available from the online companion website: resources.corwin.com/everyminutematters)

Quick Overview and Rationale

Much to my chagrin, my daughter is a very picky eater. She nibbles a little bit of this and a bite of that, as opposed to a meal being one singular entrée. I've come to realize her eating preferences are very similar to her reading style; she starts a book, reads a few pages, and moves onto the next one, before really committing to one book. I now understand that this is a reading habit that so many of us adult readers have as well; when I wander around a library or bookstore trying to select a text, I read a bit from the inside flap, a smidge from the back cover, and maybe even sample a few pages. After all, that's why Amazon offers a free sample before you commit to buying a book on your Kindle. Let's encourage this reading habit in classrooms by creating spaces for Book Tastings.

 ## Step-by-Step Directions

TEACHER MODELING

- Set up your tables so that every seat has a book in front of it, with a stack of books in the center of the table.

- Model flipping through a book purposefully, using a document camera as you think aloud. Be sure to model reading the inside flaps, outside cover, table of contents, and perhaps the opening paragraphs. As you model, project a timer so students understand that this is a short activity, typically with 3 minutes to flip through the book.

- Next, think aloud as you model filling our your Book Tasting menu. Be sure to talk through what interested you about the book. I also intentionally model tasting a book that does not appeal to me so that my students understand that it's perfectly fine to reject a book. I also am sure to demonstrate that as I fill out my menu, my concern is not mechanics. I also model gluing the completed menu into my Reader's Notebook so that it serves as a resource that I can consult to address with the inevitable "I don't know what to read next" quandary.

- I typically begin with students sampling three books, allotting 3 minutes per tasting and 3 minutes to complete menu.

STUDENT PRACTICE

- After their Book Tasting, you might have students discuss in small groups the books that ranked highly on their tastings (it's also a great way to gauge whether you need multiple copies of the same book!).

 ## Moving Forward

- Book Tastings are a great way of introducing student selections for book clubs. As they taste each book, they rate their preference for selecting that book for their club.
- Book Tastings are also fun ways to jump-start independent reports in content areas. I saw one first-grade teacher select several books about animals and have students sample them as a way to select their animal of choice for soon-to-be-completed reports.
- Use students' Book Tasting menus as a way to jump-start reading conferences, as in "Share out a book that you tasted that ranked highly."

 ## Minute Mentor

Research shows that kids often struggle knowing what to read next, so Book Tastings are a great way to proactively build students' *tsunduko*. (Do you know my new favorite word? It's Japanese for "acquired but not yet read books.") My favorite explanation for Book Tastings comes from a 2019 blog from the National Council of Teachers of English (NCTE), found here:

- https://www2.ncte.org/blog/2019/09/book-tastings

Book Tasting Menu

Rating ☐

Genre or Book Type

_____

Book Title _____

_____

_____

Who do you think of the cover?

_____

_____

After reading a few pages, what do you think of the book? ____

_____

_____

_____

_____

What did the author do to hook or interest you in the book? ____

_____

_____

_____

Would you read this book? ____

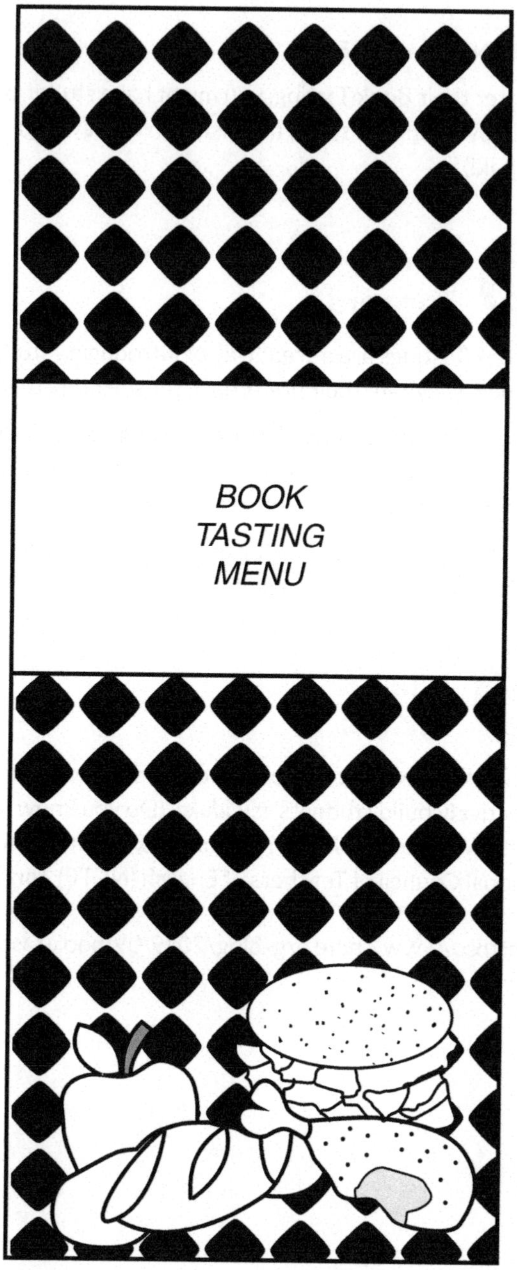

BOOK TASTING MENU

NAME _____

Set an inviting table for young readers during Book Tastings.

GO FiSH

Link to Literacy

 Listening

 Speaking

START OF DAY

Materials Needed

- Go Fish playing cards—I like to laminate mine on card stock so that I can use a dry erase marker to create lots of versions of the game (download available from the online companion website: resources.corwin.com/everyminutematters).

Quick Overview and Rationale

There are a million ways to adapt card games with a literacy twist—one of my favorite being the classic Go Fish. Kids play in small groups (ideally two to four players). Easily adaptable for many levels of students, Go Fish reinforces turn-taking and language interaction.

 ### Step-by-Step Directions

TEACHER MODELING

- Grab a teacher colleague and your document camera to demonstrate the twist on this classic card game. No other adult available? No worries—there are great videos on YouTube to show your kids how to play.

- Each player gets five cards (I might reduce this for younger kids, as their tiny hands don't have the dexterity to handle so many). The remaining cards go facedown.

- Players look at their cards and place any matches facedown. If they automatically have any matches, they may draw cards so that the game begins with all players having an equal number of cards (this also problem-solves when "shuffling" doesn't turn out so well).

- Player A asks Player B for any matching cards with a polite "Do you have any cards with ___?" If Player B has the match, she hands it to Player A. Player A puts the match aside and gets another turn.

- If Player B does not have the match, she says, "Go Fish." Player A draws from the deck. If Player A makes a match with the card drawn from the deck, she may put the match aside but does not go again.

- The game continues with turn-taking between Player A and Player B.

- The game ends when one player runs out of cards. Traditionally, the winner is the player who runs out of cards first.

Moving Forward

Here are some of my favorite adaptations for Go Fish:

- Our youngest children might Go Fish for lowercase and uppercase letters: "Jamal, do you have a lowercase *R*?"

- Children of all levels might Go Fish for sight words. Using the Fry list, the Go Fish cards have two copies of each sight word. I also like having kids use the sight word in a sentence, so "I know the answer to the math problem."

- After studying homophones, create paired cards of words that sound alike but have different meanings. Give bonus points when children use the word (e.g., When searching for the match to bare, a child might say, "Do you have the kind of bear that is an animal that lives in the woods?").

- Children in lower elementary grades might Go Fish with cards where they match picture cards to the printed word. For instance, if you've studied the -tr blend, one card has a picture of a truck and its pair has the blend (and/or word) written on it.

- I've even seen kids Go Fish where they match a character's events to the name of a character in a book that they've completed.

Minute Mentor

The team of authors from *Words Their Way: Word Study for Phonics, Vocabulary, and Spelling Instruction* (Bear, Invernizzi, Templeton, & Johnston, 2015) provide great ideas on Go Fish as a part of word study. Also, check out this article from *The Language Teacher* (Fieser, 1999) on the linguistic benefits of Go Fish for language learners:

- https://jalt-publications.org/tlt/departments/myshare/articles/2511-variations-go-fish-making-most-old-game-language-classroom

Go Fish Playing Cards

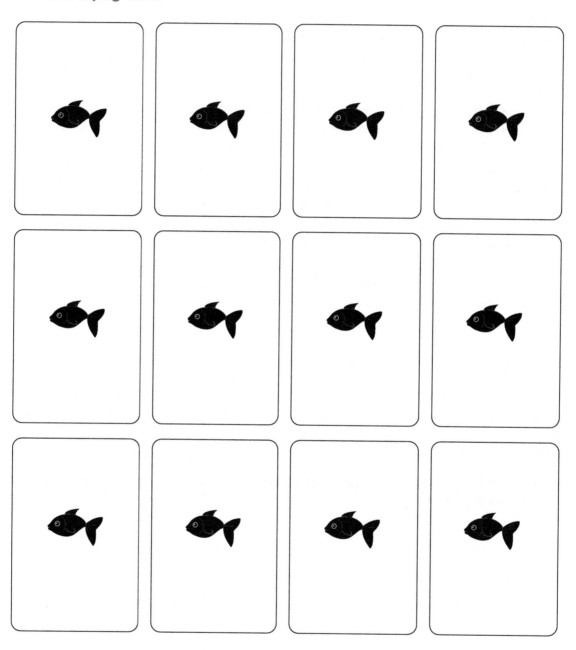

Photo by Jo Bryan

A fourth grader plays Go Fish with long vowel patterns.

CONCENTRATION

Link to Literacy

Reading

START OF DAY

Materials Needed

- Word cards (I often reuse the cards that I've created for Go Fish; download available from the online companion website: resources .corwin.com/everyminutematters)

Quick Overview and Rationale

I love Concentration because it's low prep, can be played solo or with a partner, and it supports students in building their working memory. A crucial component in executive function, working memory is a child's ability to keep information in mind and then use it in same way. You may know Concentration as "Memory" and may have played it with picture cards with very young children—so here's a literacy twist to it.

Step-by-Step Directions

- Using cards in pairs, shuffle the cards and place them facedown on a flat surface.

- A player turns two cards over. If the cards match, the player picks up the cards and keeps them.

- If the cards don't match, the player turns the cards back over. In subsequent turns, children aim to remember what they had uncovered in each turn—hence tapping into short-term memory skills.

- The game is over when all of the cards have been matched into pairs

Moving Forward

- For very young children, I reduce the number of cards. For kindergartners, I might start with only eight cards (four sets of pairs).

- Students can also play collaboratively. Here Partner A chooses a card, turns it over, and Partner B does the same. This collaboration encourages students to work together to remember the placement of each other's cards.

The versions of Concentration are similar to those of Go Fish, explained in previous pages:

- Lowercase and uppercase letters for very young children

- Print and cursive letters for children mastering cursive

- Sight words

- Homophones

- Word study patterns (e.g., ways to spell the long -a pattern with the -e marker, ai, ay)

Minute Mentor

Want to learn more about working memory, executive function, and their relationship to reading development? Here are some of my favorite resources:

- Brown, P., Roediger, H., & McDaniel, M. (2014). *Making it stick: The science of successful learning.* Cambridge, MA: Belknap Press

- Cartwright, K. (2015). *Executive skills and reading comprehension: A guide for educators.* New York, NY: Guilford Press.

iStock.com/SDI Productions

LINING UP WITH LITERACY

Link to Literacy

Speaking

Listening

Materials Needed

None

Quick Overview and Rationale

How many times in one week do your students line up to leave your classroom? Most instructional ideas prepare students to walk quietly and quickly down the hall, like the chants of "Hands on hips, zip up lips, standing tall, ready for the hall." Sure, we'd like our students to walk down the halls as silently as stealth ninjas, but have you ever tallied how much time and energy you spend in the mere process of having kids line up? How about using these times to reinforce phonological awareness and letter-sound knowledge?

Step-by-Step Directions

STUDENT PRACTICE

- PreK and K might use phonological awareness activities to line up, like "Line up if your name has one syllable. Line up if your name has three syllables, etc." In later grades, you might provide the sound of the letter, so "Line up if the second sound in your name is /e/."

- Fill a mason jar with craft sticks. On each craft stick, write a letter of the alphabet. Have students randomly take a stick, and then have them line up in alphabetical order with the craft stick that they took.

- Rhyme Time: Provide a word, and select students who can give a rhyming word to line up. For example, you might give kindergartners the word *mouse*. Call on students who can generate rhyming words—nonsense words count too! Differentiate with more difficult words (longer or multisyllabic words) or simple CVC words for students needing more support.

- For preK and K students, play Guess the Name. Rather than saying each name, spell it. When students identify their name, they line up.

- Try Alphabet Exits. Provide a category, and students must generate an example of the category in alphabetic order. For instance, if you provide "Food" as the category, a student might provide the word *avocado*. The next student might provide the word *bean* and so on in alphabetic order.

Moving Forward

- Encourage students to brainstorm their own lists about appropriate behavior both for lining up and for traveling within the school building.

Minute Mentor

Phonological awareness—a child's ability to attend to the speech sounds in language—is an essential building block of literacy. For more ideas of the importance of phonological awareness and how to incorporate it through playful activities, I recommend this article:

- Yopp, H., & Yopp, R. (2009). Phonological awareness is child's play. *Young Children*, pp. 12–21.

iStock.com/FatCamera

I SPY

Link to Literacy

 Speaking

 Listening

Materials Needed

None

Quick Overview and Rationale

We've all played I Spy—the guessing game where the "spy" locates an object and prompts the guesser to locate it with the tantalizing rhyme, "I spy with my little eye...." As the mother of a young child, I've used this low-prep game to pass many moments waiting in lines, at doctor's offices, and in various other places where the second hand seems to move backward. Typically, we use the game with preschoolers to teach colors: "I spy with my little eye something red." But who says we can't tweak this game and use it in the classroom? This quick game reinforces vocabulary, idea generation, and social skills like turn-taking. This is one of my favorite activities for those "hurry up and wait" times. By that, I mean the times that we've gotten our students in line yet are waiting for an event to unfold (for instance, waiting outside an assembly or for their turn at class photo day).

 ## Step-by-Step Directions

Speaking and listening

- Remind students that you will call on students who have raised a quiet hand.
- Use the following literacy-rich prompts to act as the spy:
  » I spy with my little eye something that rhymes with...
  » I spy with my little eye something that starts with the sound/letter/digraph/blend...

 ## Moving Forward

- To encourage partner work and conversation, put students into pairs. Each partner can whisper their guesses to each other, and then they can raise quiet hands to be called on.
- You can adapt this game easily into a sight word search. You might write a handful of sight words on the board, and during independent, guided, or shared reading, students can signal to indicate "I spy with my little eye the sight word *their.*"
- Allow students to work in small groups or table clusters to choose the "spy." Let them provide the clues and take turns being the spy and the guesser.

Minute Mentor

The I Spy concept is so popular that Scholastic has published a related series of books. Check them out (and corresponding lesson plans) on this blog post:

- https://www.scholastic.com/teachers/lesson-plans/teaching-content/i-spy-lesson-plan

iStock.com/FatCamera

CATEGORY CHAIN

Link to Literacy

Listening

Speaking

TRANSiTiON TiME

Materials Needed

None

Quick Overview and Rationale

Do you ever find yourself asking, "Are you listening to what I'm saying?" Here's a quick activity to encourage active listening, vocabulary, and retrieval practice to build memory. This game challenges students to say an answer that fits the category while listening to their classmates and remembering their answers.

This is one of my favorite activities to settle students back into seated, quiet instruction. I loved to use it when students return from gym or recess and needed a time to calm down quietly in their seats and to be ready to listen for my direction and instruction.

Step-by-Step Directions

TEACHER MODELING

- Model how to provide an example of the category. For instance, the category might be "Colors," so you might model providing the word *red* as your answer.

- The next person must say the first person's answer (thus encouraging memory and listening skills) before saying his own. So the fourth student might repeat, "red, purple, green" before providing his answer of "silver."

STUDENT PRACTICE

- Provide your students with a category (e.g., colors, animals, clothing items for cold weather). Students will give their answer to the word chain after they've provided their classmates answers.

- To prevent disengagement, you might break your class into smaller groups. For example, in a class of 20, you might have four chains of five students; this might allow for friendly competition among groups to see which group can make the longest chain.

Moving Forward

- For younger students, students who struggle with expressive language, or students with limited vocabularies, you might provide an allotted amount of time to work together to brainstorm ideas so that they are not on the spot when it's their turn. You might allow them to do quick Internet searches to generate ideas.

- For older students, you might make your categories specific, whereas categories might be broader for younger students. For instance, for a first-grade class, you might provide "Animals" as a category; for a fifth-grade class, you might give "Reptiles." Kindergartners might benefit from the broadness of "Food," whereas fourth graders might be more challenged by a narrower focus like "Food You Eat for Breakfast."

 **Minute Mentor**

An important part of learning, working memory is the ability to keep something in mind while you attend to another task. For more information about working memory—and its relationship to reading—take a look at these resources:

- https://childmind.org/article/what-is-working-memory
- https://chadd.org/wp-content/uploads/2018/06/ATTN_02_11_ImprovingMemory.pdf
- https://www.readingrockets.org/article/10-strategies-enhance-students-memory

GHOST WRITING

Link to Literacy

Writing

Materials Needed

None

Quick Overview and Rationale

Young children need lots of practice writing their letters, but there are far more engaging ways to do so than lined sheets of paper or workbook pages! I incorporate Ghost Writing as my students filed quietly down the hall; they became accustomed to my directions of "by the time you reach the far corner, be sure you've given a letter to your partner. When we stop, your partner will whisper their guess into your ear." This also helped keep my line together—so that there weren't stragglers ambling well behind the rest of the group.

Step-by-Step Directions

Give your children lots of time to practice handwriting in a variety of tactile ways:

- As they stand in line, have them "ghost write" a letter on the back of the child in front of them. Their partner guesses the letter.

- If touching a partner's back is off limits, have the partner close his eyes while the other partner ghost writes in the palm of his hand.

- Or turn this into sky writing, where they extend an arm and write the letter in the sky for their partner to guess.

Moving Forward

- Children in Grades 2 and 3 might try Ghost Writing in cursive.

Minute Mentor

When I work with teachers and parents, I often hear concerns about children's handwriting. Handwriting is, in fact, an important skill that needs explicit instruction. This Reading Rockets blog explains the importance of handwriting:

- https://www.readingrockets.org/article/importance-teaching -handwriting

This article is also useful in understanding the role of handwriting instruction in early childhood classrooms:

- Vander Hart, N., Fitzpatrick, P., & Cortesa, C. (2010). In-depth analysis of handwriting curriculum and instruction in four kindergarten classrooms. *Reading and Writing 23*, 673–699.

BUILD A WORD

Materials Needed

- List of spelling words

Quick Overview and Rationale

Spelling is often overlooked, and too often we rely on instructional practices that are disengaging or rely on rote memorization for spelling. Let's go beyond "write each spelling word three times." Here's a more engaging way to reinforce spelling words.

Step-by-Step Directions

- Say the target word aloud. For instance, the word is *trouble*.

- Students will take individual turns providing the next letter in correct sequence aloud; the first student says "T," the next says "R," and so on.

- If a student is incorrect, have him return to his spelling list and search for his error. For instance, if a student says "U" instead of "O," you might say this: "That's not quite right. Look up your list and see if you can find your own error."

- To reinforce listening skills, you might ask students to repeat each letter from the start of the word before adding on. So the first student would say "T," the second student would say "T-R," and the third would say "T-R-O," and so on.

Moving Forward

- To actively involve more students, you might have multiple chains going at once.

- Some students may be more successful with visual word chains, as opposed to an oral activity. Group students into small groups. Give each group a plastic baggie. In each bag is a stack of index cards; each index card has a letter on it. In their small groups, students work to spell the target word by placing the letter cards in the correct order. I often use these small groups as a way to subdivide the class for my whole-group time. For instance, if I've given out a plastic baggie with the word *hurt*, students would spell their word, and I can then direct them to do this: "If you were in the group that spelled *hurt*, go collect your social studies books."

- If your students are motivated by friendly competition, you might split them into teams so that they earn points for their team.

- This is also a great way to get kids to line up. Say the spelling word, and when students can provide the next correct letter, they join the line.

Minute Mentor

Here are a few of my favorite resources on effective spelling instruction:

- Palmer, J., & Invernizzi, M. (2014). *No more phonics and spelling worksheets*. Portsmouth, NH: Heinemann.

- Weakland, M. (2017). Super spellers: Seven steps to transform your spelling instruction. Portsmouth, NH: Stenhouse.

- International Literacy Association. (2019). *Teaching and assessing spelling* [Literacy leadership brief]. Newark, DE: Author.

CLASSROOM CHARADES

Link to Literacy

 Speaking

 Listening

TRANSITION time

Materials Needed

- List of possible Classroom Charades clues
- Hint: I love this website for ideas! http://www.getcharadesideas.com/resources/charades-ideas-for-kids-of-all-ages-the-ultimate-list-130-ideas

Quick Overview and Rationale

I will never forget one particularly competitive round of charades at a family game night. I come from a family of readers, so imagine my surprise—at age 8—when I had to act out the title of Newbery winner *From the Mixed Up Files of Mrs. Basil E. Frankweiler*. Fortunately, my theatrical prowess and my family's shared reading habits made for a winning combination.

Most of us are familiar with charades, the ever-popular game that challenges players to act out a clue to their teammates—without speaking or making any sounds. How about using Classroom Charades to act out vocabulary, book characters, or other practical phrases? I use Classroom Charades at the transitional times where we've got an extra few minutes and I'm sensing my kids have some energy to work off! While I wouldn't use Classroom Charades right before we start independent reading, I'd be sure to do it before the final bell is about to ring.

 ## Step-by-Step Directions

TEACHER MODELING

- Review the rules of Classroom Charades:
  » There is no talking, moving lips, or using other verbal hints while acting out a word.
  » Acting out or pantomiming similar sounding words is allowed. Show kids that tugging on their ear is charades lingo for "sounds like."
  » Set a time limit. (I like 2 minutes!)
  » The guessers of the team are allowed to ask the actor, but the actor can only confirm yes or no by nodding.
  » Any blurting of words means automatic disqualification.
- It might be helpful to show a quick YouTube video of Classroom Charades.
- Throughout the year, compile a basket of charade-worthy phrases. My preference is to have reading-focused phrases—popular book characters and titles. Be sure to be mindful of included titles or characters that you've read aloud (to ensure that all students will know them). For example, how would your students act out Harry Potter? What about the Dr. Seuss title *Green Eggs and Ham*?

- As you play, be sensitive to your students' personalities; are some students brave enough to act out *Matilda* to the entire class, or would it be more appropriate for your shyer students to work with just a partner?
- Remind children that *pantomime* means to describe with gestures and not words.

STUDENT PRACTICE

- Have students draw an idea from the basket and pantomime with gestures to get their teammates to identify the clue.
- Set a timer for 1 minute. If the clue is guessed correctly before time is up, a point is earned.

Moving Forward

- Encourage students to add their own clues to the Classroom Charades basket. As they finish books—either whole-class or independently—suggest that they add recognizable titles or notable characters as Classroom Charades clues.
- Use picture flashcards for younger players or for students who need a pictorial representation.

Minute Mentor

Some of the fun of Classroom Charades is the theatric element, and there's a whole body of research that shows that theater arts inclusion is beneficial in early childhood classrooms.

- Mages, W. (2018). The effect of drama on language, perspective-taking, and imagination. *Early Childhood Research Quarterly, 45*, 224–237.

Or check out this blog about the importance of theater in early childhood education:

https://novakdjokovicfoundation.org/using-drama-theater-classroom-promote-literacy

TELEPHONE

Link to Literacy

 Listening

 Speaking

Materials Needed

- Short phrases
- Peruse this site for ideas: https://hobbylark.com/party-games/telephone-game-phrases

Quick Overview and Rationale

Telephone is a ubiquitous childhood game! It's so popular that lovable talk show host and comedian Ellen DeGeneres features it frequently. Besides the fun factor, there are valuable literacy skills underpinning the activity; telephone reinforces the oral language, listening, and speaking components of literacy. This activity is perfect as children are lined up learning the classroom.

Step-by-Step Directions

- Jot down some fun phrases. Be sure to include alliteration, keep them short, and be silly. Incorporate the names of your students, or work in focal points of your curriculum. For instance, if you're focusing on the letter *T* and the /t/ sound in your kindergarten classroom, try out "Two tiny toads ate fat flies." Or merely write out sentences or phrases that incorporate vocabulary words or content concepts. Studying author's purpose in fourth grade? Try out "Authors write books to persuade, inform, and entertain." After a geography lesson, you could play Telephone with "The equator divides the world into the Northern Hemisphere and the Southern Hemisphere."

- Remind children that they must listen carefully, as the phrase will not be repeated.

- The first person in the line whispers a word or phrase into the ear of the person behind them. Repeat this step until the message reaches the last player in line.

- The last player says the phrase out loud so that everyone can hear how much it has changed.

Moving Forward

- Don't let the back of the line miss out on the fun! Take your line, and divide into the front half and the back half. Take the same fun phrase, and give it to the line leader and the line caboose. The front of the line will whisper to the student behind them, while the back of the line will whisper to the child ahead of them. Both halves will meet in the middle and compete to see who were better listeners.

Minute Mentor

In order to have a responsive classroom—where all students listen and hear each other—students need time to practice active listening. Check out the importance of listening skills and classroom environments in these articles:

- Brent, R., & Anderson, P. (1992). Developing children's classroom listening strategies. *The Reading Teacher, 47*, 122–126.
- Kelly, L., Ogden, M., & Moses, L. (2019). Speaking and listening in the primary grades. *Young Children, 74*.

iStock.com/FatCamera

WOULD YOU RATHER?

Link to Literacy

 Speaking

 Listening

TRANSITION time

Materials Needed

- List of questions that pose options for students to ponder (Hint: The questions should be fun, engaging, and—yes—even sometimes gross! Each question must present a pair of options; these options should either be equally positive or equally negative.)

- Or try out some options from this website: https://conversationstartersworld.com/would-you-rather-questions-for-kids Or try this one: https://www.thebestideasforkids.com/would-you-rather-questions-for-kids

Quick Overview and Rationale

In the console of my car, I keep Sunny Panda's (2019) book *Would You Rather Book For Kids: The Book of Silly Scenarios, Challenging Choices, and Hilarious Situations the Whole Family Will Love (Game Book Gift Ideas)*. This book has kept my young daughter and I giggling as we waited at restaurants, in traffic jams, and even at the DMV. As we ponder gross questions like "Would you rather lick a dirty trash can or lick the bathroom floor?" or creative ones like "Would you rather be invisible or be able to fly?," we are actually engaging in literacy skills (without her knowing!)—we take a stance, we defend our position, and we listen to and consider each other's points of view, all in the name of presenting a solid argument or defense. All of these skills are essential in the classroom, particularly in conjunction with instruction in opinion writing.

 ## Step-by-Step Directions

TEACHER MODELING

- Choose a question to model and think aloud to model and internally debate it. I might choose a question that is simple and fun, such as "Would you rather have a pool or a trampoline?" Talk through the pros and cons of each option to model your thought process before ultimately deciding on one.

- You might even model drafting a quick T chart to show your thinking; while I don't expect students to use their own T charts, it may help them understand the thinking process.

STUDENT PRACTICE

- After posing a question, give students 1 minute to think though their answer before doing a Turn and Talk. I use a 1-1-1 approach here: 1 minute to brainstorm answer, 1 minute to actively listen to a partner, 1 minute to explain their choice.

- Allow students who are ready to share their answers with the class. You might even take a class poll.

Moving Forward

- Incorporate vocabulary words from content classes. For instance, after a science lesson, students might debate "Would you rather be in a hurricane or cyclone?" After a lesson about powerful word choice and verbs, they might ponder "Would you rather walk briskly or sprint?"

- Have students generate their own questions. This entails that they understand presenting two options of equal weight.

- Students might generate a written response to a particularly juicy "Would you rather?"

Minute Mentor

Persuasive argumentation is an important skill to build in childhood classrooms, as children learn to formulate an argument, use text-based evidence to defend it, and incorporate effective tools in their persuasive writing. These articles highlight how being aware of audience is a key to young children's persuasive writing:

- Burkhalter, N. (1995). Vygotsky-based curriculum for teaching persuasive writing in the elementary grades. *Language Arts, 72,* 192–199.

- Wollman-Bonilla, J. (2000). *Family message journals: Teaching writing through family involvement.* Urbana, IL: National Council of Teachers of English.

HiNK PiNKS

Materials Needed

- Clue cards; clues are provided below

Quick Overview and Rationale

Phonological awareness is a foundational literacy skill, but it's far more effective when it's taught through engaging activities. Can you think of a pair of rhyming words that describe an overweight feline? Did you get "fat cat"? That's a Hink Pink! Hink Pinks are one-syllable words that rhyme—a fun way to incorporate phonological awareness and vocabulary. You provide the definition, and kids generate the pair of rhyming words that meet the clue. Other terms for Hink Pinks are Brain Trains or Wordy Gurdies. There are endless Hink Pinks available, so I've listed just a few. You'll find many more in basic Internet searches.

 Step-by-Step Directions

TEACHER MODELING

- Tell students that you will be playing a word game. Tell them that their jobs are to listen to the clues and to provide two rhyming words that match the clues.

- Begin with simple Hink Pinks with lower-level vocabulary. For example, you might say, "I'm looking for two rhyming words that describe a large feline."

- Do not allow students to shout out their responses but to give a thumbs-up to indicate that they've got it.

- For the first several Hink Pinks, model your thinking in how you arrived at the answer. For example, you might say, "Another word for *feline* is a *cat*. If I try to come up with a rhyming word for *cat*, that also matches the clue of *heavy*: I get the rhyming pair *fat cat*. So my Hink Pink is *fat cat*." You might also call on a student and prompt them: "Don't tell us the answer, but walk us through how you got the answer, step-by-step."

- For an additional level of support, you might provide the first letters of the answer. So you might say, "My Hink Pink for a large feline begins with FC."

STUDENT PRACTICE

- When they've got the hang of Hink Pinks, students might be ready for Hinker Pinkers, which are two-syllable words in a rhyming pair. Here are some to try out (see the chart below).

- When they've mastered two syllables, maybe they are ready to play with Hinkety Pinketies—or three-syllable clues, also listed below.

Moving Forward

I also love having students generate their own Hink Pinks. What a great way to differentiate! To have students write their own Hink Pinks, follow these steps:

- Model how you start by thinking of the rhyming pair first. You might say, "I'm going to start with two words that rhyme: fat cat. I want to write a clue to help people guess fat cat. So maybe I think of other words—or synonyms—for *fat*. I might even use a dictionary here. I know another way to say *fat* is *obese*, so I'll use that. And now I need to think of a clue to get to *cat*. I could think of a famous cat that most people might know—like Garfield. Or I could also give another word for cat—like *feline*. So my clue would be 'an overweight feline' to get people to guess 'fat cat.'"

Minute Mentor

- For more support, check out the following link: http://www.readwritethink.org/resources/resource.print.html?id=30651

List of Clues and Corresponding Hink Pinks

Clue	Hink Pink	Clue	Hinker Pinker
A large branch	big twig	A magical woman who milks cows	dairy fairy
A movie that women like to see	chick flick	A rabbit with a sense of humor	funny bunny
A library thief	book crook	A fruit that needs a shave	hairy berry
An enjoyable jog	fun run	A tired flower	lazy daisy
A voyage that a sailboat might go on	ship trip	A big hill that spits out water	fountain mountain
24 hours of clouds	gray day	A magical reptile	wizard lizard
A hairpiece for a hog	pig wig	A smelly finger	stinky pinky
A damp plane	wet jet	A chocolate bar dropped on the beach	sandy candy

Clue	Hink Pink	Clue	Hinkety-Pinkety
A male who is golden from the sun	tan man	A place where the national leader lives	president's residence
A high fence	tall wall		
A man who is timid	shy guy	Two drums conversing with each other at a jazz concert	percussion discussion
An awful father	bad dad		
A serpent dessert	snake cake	An evil priest	sinister minister
A home for a rodent	mouse house		
A noisy group	loud crowd		
Turquoise footwear	blue shoe	A happier canine	merrier terrier
Frog street	toad road		
When a baby cow giggles	calf laugh		

Notes

HUMAN HUNGRY HiPPOS

Link to Literacy

 Reading

ANY TiME

Materials Needed

- Folded scraps of paper (placed in the center of the ring) with clues written on them
- Baskets—for the hippos to chomp with

Quick Overview and Rationale

Indoor recess again? Too rainy or cold to let kids burn off some steam outdoors? Push your desks to the side and play Human Hungry Hippos! Remember the classic 1980s board game where plastic hippopotamuses chomped marbles in a frenzy. Here's an ELA twist on that!

 ### Step-by-Step Directions

TEACHER MODELING

- I'll admit it—I still remember this jingle from the 1980s. Show your students this quick vintage commercial to familiarize them with the game: https://www.youtube.com/watch? v=Uxm3sUy1_eA
- Decide what your hippos are going to chomp; they could chomp words with phonics features that you are studying, vocabulary words and so on. Kindergartners might chomp letters, first graders might chomp CVC words, and so forth.
- Write what the hippos are chomping on small index cards. Put them into the center of your play area.
- Group your students into teams; I usually use four teams.
- Explain the rules to students:
  » One hippo moves forward to grab a card. Have your children do the wheelbarrow walk where one child holds her partner's feet while the partner walks forward on hands.
  » The hippos move forward, grab a card, bring it back to their side, and must do the literacy task on the card (e.g., read the word, say the sound, give a rhyming word, provide a synonym).
  » Use a timer to count down short time intervals; I like 3-minute intervals where kids grab as many cards as they can and do the literacy task to earn points for their team.

STUDENT PRACTICE

- Take turns rotating hippos; the game is about speed as hippos try to chomp as many cards possible for their team.

Moving Forward

- Be warned! Kids love this activity, so it's a perfect incentive for the class to earn. Better yet, let them create the cards as teachers or administrators become the hippos. (Admit it! You sort of want to play too!)

- There are ample opportunities for differentiation here; cards might be different colors to indicate different levels (without students' knowledge), and teams are designated to chomp certain colors.

- Students who cannot participate in the physicality of the game might be scorekeepers or check to make sure that each team is on top of the literacy task.

Minute Mentor

A 2017 study shows the effectiveness of using board games with instructional adaptations in the classroom. The study revealed that board games help students be active but also increase motivation, cooperation, and joy for students (Gerovasiliou & Zafiri, 2017).

SPELLING CONNECT FOUR

Link to Literacy

Reading

ANY TIME

Materials Needed

- Connect Four Board (download available from the online companion website: resources.corwin.com/everyminutematters)

- I like to glue a few paper copies onto a manila folder and laminate the entire thing; this allows me to use a dry erase marker and instantly make a new board.

- Chips or tokens to use as game pieces

- Dice

Quick Overview and Rationale

In case you've forgotten, Connect Four is the old favorite that challenges players to be the first to get four colored checkers in a row either horizontally, vertically, or diagonally. It's a great game for strategy, pattern recognition, planning skills, and problem solving. With a bit of imagination and some clear tape, Connect Four becomes a great literacy game.

Spelling Connect Four

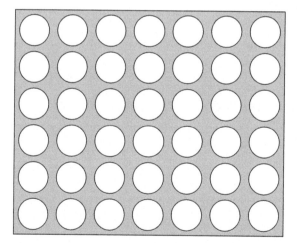

 Step-by-Step Directions

- Each player chooses a color token.

- Players take turns rolling a die, choosing a word in that column, saying the word, and placing a marker on the space if said correctly.

- If the student reads a word and can't find a place for it on the board, they lose their turn.
- The first player to connect four in a row wins!

Moving Forward

The simple version was just given, but there are many ways to differentiate. For younger students, you might have the boards have letter names or word families. Older students might have sight words or multisyllabic words. Another option is to use a dry erase marker to write the target spelling features on the board and give students a stack of word cards. Stack the word cards upside down, and have students draw one at a time. They aim to read the word aloud and place it on top of the correct square. So in the blends version pictured below, a student picks up the word *grass*, they must correctly read the word in order to be able to claim the /gr/ box. They would then choose any of the /gr/ squares to place their token.

Connect Four

cr	sl	br	gr	sp
sn	cl	bl	fl	sn
cl	cr	br	cr	bl
sp	dr	gr	sp	cl
sn	sl	dr	bl	sp
br	sp	gr	cl	cr

Minute Mentor

For more great ideas on spelling and word study games, check out some of my favorite resources:

- Bear, D., Invernizzi, M., Templeton, S., & Johnston, F. (2015). *Words their way: Word study for phonics, vocabulary, and spelling instruction.* New York, NY: Pearson.
- Koutrakos, P. (2019). *Word study that sticks: Best practices K-6.* Thousand Oaks, CA: Corwin Press.
- Weakland, M. (2017). *Super spellers: Seven steps to transforming your spelling instruction.* Portsmouth, NH: Stenhouse.

VOCABULARY VASE

Link to Literacy

Speaking

Listening

Materials Needed

- Glass jar
- Paper strips with previously discussed words written on them

Quick Overview and Rationale

Isn't it frustrating when you teach rich vocabulary words only to find students not using them in subsequent weeks? With the Vocabulary Vase, students revisit previously taught words as the teacher pulls out words.

 ### Step-by-Step Directions

TEACHER MODELING

- Write out a select number of words on paper strips, and add them to the Vocabulary Vase.
- Randomly select a word from the Vocabulary Vase.
- In a think aloud, model how you define the word, describe the word, give an example, or use it in a sentence. For instance, if the word is *ravenous*, you might say, "I know that ravenous means really hungry, so I could answer, 'My stomach rumbled when I felt ravenous.'"

STUDENT PRACTICE

- Call for a volunteer to define the word, describe it, give examples, or use it in a sentence.
- If multiple students volunteer, they might work in small groups or partners to exchange definitions or sentences.
- This can easily be adapted as a transitional strategy, with students lining up once they've proven their understanding of a word.
- For students who struggle, you might provide the word in a sentence starter, and they fill in the sentence. For example, if a student struggles to define the word *drowsy*, you might give the sentence starter of "I could tell she felt drowsy because…"

 ### Moving Forward

- Rotate words every 4 weeks so that the Vocabulary Vase is constantly changing.
- Call out two words, and challenge students to incorporate them into one sentence.

ANY TIME

Minute Mentor

The importance of vocabulary knowledge cannot be understated; students with strong vocabularies outperform their peers on measures of reading comprehension (Stanovich, 1986). Additionally, research shows that students need multiple exposures to words as well as revisiting words over time in order to cement them in their lexicons (Beck, McKeown, & Kucan, 2013; Cobb & Blachowicz, 2014).

iStock.com/Wavebreakmedia

BOOK PASS

Link to Literacy

Reading

Speaking

ANY TIME

Materials Needed

- Lots and lots of books—Carol Jago (2018) suggests needing three times as many books as students. Be sure to include a wide variety of text genre, format, levels, and so on.

Quick Overview and Rationale

Too many of our children have never had the pleasure of wandering aimlessly through a bookstore. So let's simulate the magic in that experience, and simulate it in the classroom! One of my favorite activities to do when I've got extra time in my classroom is a Book Pass, which aims to provide lots of exposure of lots of titles to students in a short time. This is a slight modification of some of the previous activities, like Library Love and Book Tasting. There's very little preparation necessary other than gathering titles that might appeal to your students

Step-by-Step Directions

TEACHER MODELING

- Model with a stack of books of different length and varying genre, thinking aloud to show why the book appeals to me (or why it doesn't). Use language like this:
  - » Here's something that interests me about this book....
  - » This book doesn't look like quite the right one for me because...
  - » This book might be interesting because...

- Model for five books before giving students time to try on their own. Of those five books, I'm sure to pass on some books but use nonjudgmental language.

STUDENT PRACTICE

- Randomly place a book on each student's desk (I like to do this while my students are out of the room so that they return to a new title at their seats).

- Tell students that they have 1 minute to flip through the book (I display the time on my SMART Board using Google Timer). Direct students to peruse the back cover, the illustrations, the inside flap, the table of contents, and any other appealing text features.

- At the end of 1 minute, tell students that they can either hold on to the book (signifying that it's a book they'd like to add to their independent reading collection) or they can pass it along to a classmate. If a student chooses to keep a book, replace it with another book. Continue through a few more rounds.

- After four or five passes, I like to call a time out to allot time for conversation. This can either be whole-class, small-group (in tables), or even in partners. Encourage students to reflect on these questions:
  - » Showcase any texts you've kept. Why did you choose to keep them?
  - » What features were appealing to you?
  - » What made you decide the book was worth keeping?
  - » For students who have not kept any texts, have them explain what they are looking for, why they passed on other texts, and what did not appeal to them in the texts they've looked at.
  - » Explain that the goal is not for everyone to select a book (I don't always find a book when I go to my public library). Rather, the aim is to build their capacities to browse through books and to better know their reading identities (and what appeals to them).

Moving Forward

- If your school has media center or library, a recap of the Book Pass is a great way to start your library visits. Ask students to remember how to browse through a book and how to decide on what they'd like to read.

- I also like to use Book Passes as a way to jump-start my reading conferences with students. I might begin with "Tell me about your Book Pass experience. Did you find anything? What did you learn about yourself as a reader?"

Minute Mentor

Have you read *The Book in Question: Why and How Reading Is in Crisis* by Carol Jago (2018)? I've adapted Book Pass from Jago's work, who states, "I'm sure I learned about this from another teacher but have long forgotten from whom. If it was you, I apologize and hereby offer credit" (p. 7) Authors Donalyn Miller and Colby Sharp credit book passes to Janet Allen's (2000) *Yellow Brick Road: Shared and Guided Paths to Independent Reading*.

PARKING LOT

Link to Literacy

 Speaking

 Writing

Materials Needed

- Sticky notes
- Portion of classroom wall

Quick Overview and Rationale

I'll admit it. I'm somewhat obsessed with the questions that kids ask. My fascination with student-generated questions began when my daughter was 4 years old, and every morning I was bombarded with a barrage of whys. With a bit of digging, I discovered that children ages 2 to 10 ask an average of 288 questions a day (Frazier, Gelman, & Wellman, 2009)! Yet in formal schooling, there seems to be little time (or priority) for children's curiosity, as teachers do far more of the questioning. When we carve instructional time and space to honor children's questions, powerful things happen; check out my article *The Question Is the Answer* (Ness, 2015) for evidence.

But let's be real. Some of the questions that students generate are untimely, off topic, inappropriate, or just leave us scratching our heads for an answer and an origin. Create a Parking Lot in your classroom as an anytime catchall for kids' questions. Harmin and Toth (2006) explain that the Parking Lot "reminds us to handle such deferred questions, assures students that their questions will not be forgotten, and, of course, helps us to keep our lessons flowing with active involvement" (p. 219).

 ## Step-by-Step Directions

TEACHER MODELING

- Section off a space on your classroom wall as the "Parking Lot." If you're crafty, enjoy decorating it!

- The next time a student asks a question that is off topic, difficult to answer, or you don't have immediate time to answer, praise his curiosity and explain that the question is perfect for the Parking Lot. Tell your students that the Parking Lot is a place to store their questions that cannot immediately be answered. Explain that those questions will be answered at a later point.

- Model writing the question on a sticky note. Create a designated spot for sticky notes. Have students jot their initials on the backs of their sticky notes as a record of who posed the question.

STUDENT PRACTICE

- Encourage students to add questions to the Parking Lot as they generate questions in reading, in content-area conversations, from informational text, and from their natural wonderings.

- As time allows, visit the Parking Lot as a whole class and search for answers on Internet searches and through texts. You might even designate a portion of the Parking Lot for answers to their questions, as shown in the "I learned…" part shown in the photo.

Moving Forward

- Act as a scribe for younger students or students who struggle to write their questions.
- Use the Parking Lot questions as a perfect transition for selecting text at the classroom or school library. For instance, when a third grader asked me "If we have a Big Dipper and a Little Dipper, why don't we have a Medium Dipper?" we used that question to guide our text selection on constellations.

Minute Mentor

For more ideas and uses of the Parking Lot, check out two of my articles:

- Ness, M. (2013). Unpark those questions. *Educational Leadership, 71,* 74–76.
- Ness, M. (2014). Moving student-generated questions out of the parking lot. *The Reading Teacher, 67,* 369–373.

In this photo, the teacher has split the I Wonder wall into two parts, "I Wonder" and "I Learned," so students can note questions then research and share what they've discovered.

SiNK OR SPELL

ANY TiMe

Link to Literacy

 Writing

 Speaking

Materials Needed

- Sink or Spell board (download available from the online companion website: resources.corwin.com/everyminutematters)
- List of familiar spelling words
- Dry erase markers

Quick Overview and Rationale

As a child, I spent many rainy afternoons in the lodge of my summer camp playing Battleship. Remember this classic game? You placed your plastic battleship in pegs on a board that your opponent could not see. The goal was to sink your opponent's ships using the horizontal and vertical coordinates as your guides. You'd guess "B1." Your opponent would respond with either "hit" or "miss." If you got a miss, you'd mark your incorrect guess with a white peg. If you got a hit, you'd mark the spot with a red peg and continue guessing in that area until you sunk the ship. Here's a fun twist to that game—only this time students use their spelling and/or vocabulary words as their "ships."

 ## Step-by-Step Directions

TEACHER MODELING

- Prep a file folder, and glue two sheets on the inside facing each other: the sheet titled "My Words" is where Player A writes out her words, and the sheet titled "My Guesses" is where Player A marks her guesses. Laminate the entire folder so that it is reusable (students use a washable dry erase marker). Students play in pairs, so each partner needs their own folder (see photo).

- Each player brings his list of vocabulary or spelling words to play; I recommend using words that are somewhat familiar (this makes a great review activity before a spelling assessment).

- Both players secretly choose five spelling words and write them on their My Words grid. Words may be written horizontally or vertically—or diagonally to make it more challenging for older players—but not backward. Words may touch each other, but they cannot overlap.

- Players take turns calling out coordinates (e.g., C7). If a player's opponent has a letter in the corresponding box, the opponent says "hit" and tells the other player what letter is in the box. If the box is empty, the opponent says "miss." If it was a hit, the player who made the shot writes the letter on the My Guesses grid at the proper coordinates. If it was a miss, the player marks the box with an X.

- If there is a hit, the player may guess the word or use her turns to continue to guess coordinates. If the word was correct, the player must spell the word correctly. If the word is spelled correctly, the opponent will say, "You sunk my (spelling word)!" If the word was not guessed correctly or not spelled correctly, it counts as a miss.

Moving Forward

- In the beginning of the year, I use this game to have my students learn to spell each other's names.
- I also use this version of Sink or Spell as a way to practice sight words!

Minute Mentor

Here's another great resource for spelling or word study instruction:

- Palmer, J., & Invernizzi, M. (2014). *No more phonics and spelling worksheets*. Portsmouth, NH: Heinemann.

A student prepares her board to play Sink or Spell with a classmate.

Photo by Jo Bryan

Sink or Spell

	0	1	2	3	4	5	6
A							
B							
C							
D							
E							
F							
G							
H							
I							
J							
K							

	0	1	2	3	4	5	6
A							
B							
C							
D							
E							
F							
G							
H							
I							
J							
K							

My words _____

My guesses _____

Notes

HEADBANDS

Link to Literacy

 Speaking

 Reading

Materials Needed

- Sentence strips
- List of vocabulary words
- Timer

Quick Overview and Rationale

Are you one of the millions of viewers who laugh aloud at talk show host Ellen DeGeneres and her games? Here's a twist on a particularly fun one—she calls it Heads Up. It's also a popular family board game called Hedbanz. The premise is simple: Players can't see a word that is written on their forehead (in our classroom version, I use sentence strips as headbands). A teammate gives them clues until they're able to guess the word.

 ## Step-by-Step Directions

TEACHER MODELING

- Write five different vocabulary words on five index cards.

- Have one student select one (without me knowing which word he's chosen). I hold that mystery word up to my forehead and tell students that they cannot tell me the word but that they can give me clues to help me guess the word.

- If you have younger students, it's helpful to model or play Version #1, where players can give each other clues to get them to guess their word.

- If you are playing Version #1, encourage students to give their teammates clues such as the following:
  » Parts of speech
  » Synonyms
  » Antonyms
  » Examples of the word
  » Characteristics of the word

- For instance, if the word is *aggravated*, a clue might be "This is a synonym for irritated."

- My older or more proficient students might be ready for Version #2, where players can ask their teammates any type of questions about their word with the goal of guessing it. This version is more challenging because it requires children to categorize their thinking from broad to narrow. Here the guesser is asking yes/no questions to guess the word.

- If you're playing Version #2, it's helpful to display a list of questions that your students might ask. Here are some examples:
  » Am I an action word?
  » Do I describe something?

> » Am I a place?
> » Am I an object?
> » Am I a feeling?

STUDENT PRACTICE

- On sentence strips (or use an index card and a rubber band), display somewhat familiar vocabulary words to students.

- Each player then takes a headband and adjusts it around his or her head. Be sure the word is in the center of his forehead, aligned with eyebrows, so that the student cannot see his word.

- Players earn a point by guessing the word before time runs out. Players can keep track of the points that they've earned.

Moving Forward

- Adjust the time to make it shorter or longer for your students.

- Have students brainstorm questions that they plan to ask before starting the timer.

Minute Mentor

Don't forget that study (Gerovasiliou & Zafiri, 2017) that shows the instructional benefits of board games, especially when it comes to vocabulary knowledge.

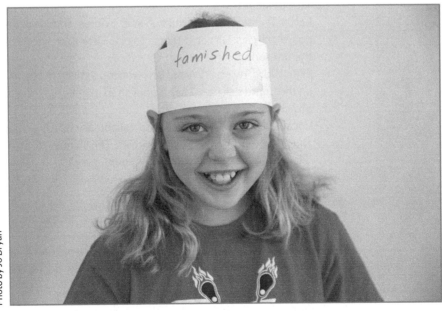

Photo by Jo Bryan

TWISTER

Link to Literacy

 Reading

 Listening

Materials Needed

- Twister board (available at any retail outlet) OR make your own Twister board from a 4 ft × 5 ft drop cloth
- Sticky notes
- Twister spinner (there's really an app for that!)

Quick Overview and Rationale

Twister is a great classroom game that will have your students laughing until they fall over. Best used in small groups, it's perfect for indoor recess or those times when your kids just need to burn off some steam! Choose from any of the variations I've provided, or create your own (and share them with me on social media with #everyminutematters).

 Step-by-Step Directions

- Spread out the board on the floor, and decide who will be the spinner. No more than five children play at a time; I also recommend no shoes!
- Players line up on opposite edges of the board. The spinner will spin and direct the players to put a certain limb (right hand, right leg, left hand, or left leg) on a certain color (red, yellow, green, or blue). However, instead of colors here, the students put their limbs on particular words or letters. Students aim to keep their limbs on each circle until directed to move it again; the player who stays balanced upright longest wins!
  - » Letter Twister: Write letters on sticky notes, and place them on the board's circles. Direct students to place a limb on the letter that makes the /m/ sound.
  - » Sight Word Twister: Write sight words on sticky notes, and place them on the board's circles. The spinner then might say, "Put your left hand on *because*."
  - » Vocabulary Word Twister: Write vocabulary words on sticky notes, and place them on the board's circles. The spinner directs players to "place your leg on the word that means *angry*."

 Moving Forward

- Advance warning: Kids love this activity, so it's a perfect incentive for the class to earn. Better yet, give them a pack of sticky notes, and challenge them to come up with their own variation.
- Students who cannot participate in the physicality of the game might be scorekeepers or be the spinner.

Minute Mentor

Research shows that movement and kinesthetic activities during the school day help students focus on learning. Check out this blog:

https://www.edutopia.org/article/research-tested-benefits-breaks

Or check out this great chapter—"Movement and Learning"—taken from Eric Jensen's (2005) *Teaching With the Brain in Mind* and available online:

http://www.ascd.org/publications/books/104013/chapters/Movement-and-Learning.aspx

Photo by Jo Bryan

LETTER FORMATION

Link to Literacy

Writing

ANY TiME

Materials Needed

- A variety of tactile materials (most found at an art supply store):
  » Wax craft sticks (e.g., Wikki Stix)
  » Play dough
  » Kinetic sand
  » Window markers

Quick Overview and Rationale

Young children need all sorts of reinforcement to develop the fluency, automaticity, and fine motor skills required in handwriting and letter formation. These activities—often found in recommendations provided by occupational therapists—are far more engaging than tracing letters on lined paper.

Step-by-Step Directions

This activity—geared toward our primary students—does not require a lot of explanation but invites them to form letters in a variety of different ways.

- Place a tarp on the floor, and invite a number of children to use their bodies to lie down and make each letter. For instance, have two children lie diagonally—with their heads touching at the top—and a third child lying midway between them to form the letter A. Capital letters here work best, and be sure to rotate helpers so that no one gets left out.

- Place a small dollop of shaving cream on student desks or tables, and have them trace letters with a cotton swab. I use a cotton swab rather than fingers to keep this activity as mess-free as possible and to be sensitive to sensory issues of some children. (Bonus: Shaving cream removes dingy pencil stains from desks.)

- At a dollar store or a party store, buy finger lights (see photo below). Project each letter on your SMART Board, and have them trace the letters with their finger lights.

- Have students form letters using a variety of art materials. My favorites are pipe cleaners or wax craft sticks, play dough, or kinetic sand (I love this stuff as it never dries out, but be sure to put it in a tray or cookie sheet to contain the mess), even window markers (yes, they really do come off of glass with glass cleaner).

- Make sensory sandwich bags by filling a plastic baggie with cheap hair gel and glitter. Double bag it, duct tape it closed, and have children write their letters in the squishiness.

Moving Forward

Once students have started to master formation, a natural next step is two-letter blends and short sight words. Or have them pair up and ask one student to speak a word and the partner to form its starting letter or ending letter. This reinforces phonological awareness, too.

Minute Mentor

Check out this article, all about the importance of handwriting:

- Vander Hart, N., Fitzpatrick, P., & Cortesa, C. (2010). In-depth analysis of handwriting curriculum and instruction in four kindergarten classrooms. *Reading and Writing, 23,* 673–699.

Photo by Jo Bryan

SiGHT WORD SeaRCH

Link to Literacy

Reading

ANY TiMe

Materials Needed

- Age-appropriate reading materials in a variety of genres. I love to use menus, kids' magazines and periodicals (like *Time for Kids* or *Highlights*), short stories, and so on.

- Magnifying glasses

Quick Overview and Rationale

Typically kids learn sight words through rote memorization and flash cards. Too often, they can read sight words from lists in isolation, yet they struggle to read the words when they encounter them in authentic text. Perhaps this is because the rote memorization focuses too much on the visual representation of the word and overlooks other aspects. To overcome this obstacle, I've tried to connect sight words to text more frequently by having kids search for words in text—kind of a literacy scavenger hunt!

 ## Step-by-Step Directions

TEACHER MODELING

- Draw explicit attention to sight words in text. For very young students, I circle them in our morning message. For students of all levels, I think aloud by saying that "I see another sight word in this book" during guided reading and shared reading.

STUDENT PRACTICE

- Using a page of their Reader's Notebook, have students write down four to six sight words; these should be sight words that are familiar and are likely to appear in text.

- Have them use a magnifying glass to be a detective and search for those words in their text.

- When they encounter the sight words in the materials they've used for hunting, have them place a tally mark next to the word in their notebook.

- I usually give students 5 minutes to complete a sight word search.

- For students who need more support, I quickly scan a text and use a sticky note to mark pages when I've predetermined the appearance of the words. This saves them the frustration of wandering through a text and not finding any of the preselected words.

Moving Forward

- Encourage your students to keep a sight word tally in their Reader's Notebooks, where they record the sight words that they've encountered.

Minute Mentor

In their 2018 gem, authors Amanda Rawlins and Marcia Invernizzi argue that sight words stick when we teach their meaning, pronunciation, and spelling. Check out more of their ideas in this article:

- Rawlins, A., & Invernizzi, M. (2018). Reconceptualizing sight words: Building an early reading vocabulary. *The Reading Teacher, 72,* 711–719.

Photo by Jo Bryan

Link to Literacy

 Writing

 Reading

ANY TIME

Materials Needed

- Repurpose an old table (34 in. by 34 in.) into a giant Scrabble board, using electrical tape to create the grid. Use wooden planks (available at your local art or hardware store) or cardboard squares to create your letters.

- In an English Scrabble board, there are 15 rows and 15 columns as well as 100 tiles in the following frequency:

» 12 E	» 4 U	» 2 V
» 9 A	» 4 D	» 2 V
» 9 I	» 3 G	» 2 Y
» 8 O	» 2 B	» 1 K
» 6 N	» 2 C	» 1 J
» 6 R	» 2 M	» 1 X
» 6 T	» 2 P	» 1 Q
» 4 L	» 2 F	» 1 Z
» 4 S	» 2 H	

Quick Overview and Rationale

Upon entering my favorite public library, you stroll past a huge table that has been fashioned into a makeshift Scrabble game. At the bottom of the table are wooden letter tiles—each roughly the size of a coaster. Library patrons are invited to play along and add a word to the ongoing game; each morning, the board is cleared by the librarian, who starts a new game by placing out a single word (albeit a lengthier word). As the day goes on, patrons amble by, pick up tiles, and add to the community Scrabble game. Why not replicate this idea for your classroom to encourage ongoing wordplay? There's no need to keep score or to count up double points squares; everyone who plays here is a winner!

 ## Step-by-Step Directions

TEACHER MODELING

- Start at the beginning of the year by showcasing Scrabble with your students' names. Using a think aloud, I model choosing a long name (or my first and last name combined) to start playing. Then, I talk through how I add on both vertically and horizontally until I've got a Scrabble board of student names.

- Invite students to share where words could be added. Usually, I snap a photo of our result and print out that photo so that students have a visual reminder of how Scrabble looks (it helps them remember that words cannot go backward or diagonally!)

- Begin our new Scrabble board with a longer word ripe with many vowels (my personal favorite starting word is *question*, as all students know it and it has many starting places!)

STUDENT PRACTICE

- As time allows, I invite students up to the Letter Tile Table to build words or add onto words (see photo below). It's perfectly acceptable to change the word *question* into *questioning* by adding the -ing (in fact, it demonstrates students' understandings of morphemes and inflected endings).

- When students are stuck, I might select tiles for them and point them in the right direction, like "Show me a CVC word that you can build off of the A, using the letters B and G."

- For simplicity's sake, I don't worry about point values for letter tiles or the colored squares on a Scrabble board for extra points.

Moving Forward

- Have no extra room in your classroom for a table? How about transforming part of your wall into a makeshift Scrabble board? On butcher paper (or on a dry erase board itself), draw a board and use sticky notes as your letter tiles.

Minute Mentor

I love this blog post from the Boys and Girls Club of Central Texas, which explains the benefits of Scrabble: https://www.bgctx.org/blog/Benefits-Of-Playing-Scrabble

Or check out this CBS News story: https://www.cbsnews.com/news/the-benefits-of-scrabble

TOWER TUMBLE

Link to Literacy

 Speaking

 Listening

Materials Needed

- Colored labels (1 in. × 2.75 in.)
- Your own label maker
- Complete set of Jenga blocks

Quick Overview and Rationale

Remember Jenga? Build a tower of wooden blocks, and ever so carefully, remove blocks and add them to the top—but don't make the tower tumble! Jenga is so popular that there is even a lawn version of it, complete with large blocks. Knowing the dimensions of the typical blocks (1.5 in. × 2.5 in. × 7.5 in.) opens up tons of possibilities—using a label maker, a permanent marker, or printing labels from your computer. Here are just a few ideas to adapt Jenga into a literacy-rich version of Tower Tumble.

 ## Step-by-Step Directions

Tower Tumble has super easy rules: Partners takes turns gently removing one block at a time from any level of the tower. They then place it on the topmost level in order to complete it. The game ends when the tower falls—completely or if any block falls from the tower (other than the block a player moves on a turn). To add a literacy twist, here are just a few ideas:

- Write vocabulary words on each block. As students pull a block, they must define the word and use it in a sentence.
- Write sight words or homophones on each block, having students read them and use them in a sentence.

 ## Moving Forward

This game is even possible with our youngest students, though I might reduce the number of blocks to make it easier for their tiny hands. Blocks might have a letter on them, with students having to name the letter, produce its sound, and provide a word starting with the letter. As they progress, they might be ready for word families to be written on each block. To use this across the content areas, you might write key terms from science or social studies, and children have to explain them. I've even seen teachers use Tower Tumble as a way to scaffold oral language for English language learners. A student pulls a block with an open-ended question, like "What is the best movie you've seen?" and their partner must answer.

Minute Mentor

There are so many different variations on how to use Tower Tumble as a center, as a review game, and as an icebreaker. Check out some of the fun ideas on this blog:

- http://eslcarissa.blogspot.com/2014/05/jenga-in-classroom.html

My social media buddy Paul Hankins cuts out words from magazines and decoupages them onto Jenga blocks so that students generate Jenga poetry. Read about it here:

- http://paulwhankins.edublogs.org

CHECKERS

Link to Literacy

 Speaking

 Listening

Materials Needed

- Basic checkerboard
- Dot stickers (small sticky notes will work in a pinch!)

Quick Overview and Rationale

I love this activity as a way to have kids work in partners to generate sentences with words that are essential for their understanding and knowledge. There are multiple benefits for Checkers: concentration, problem solving, advance planning, and memory planning. All of these possibilities are amplified with an easy literacy twist.

Step-by-Step Directions

- Take 12 dot stickers, and write a different noun or verb on each one. Stick the dot stickers on checkers.
- Checkers can only move on black squares and move diagonally forward one space at a time.
- On the first move, players can move two spaces.
- The goal is for players to move their checkers to the other side of the board in order to be "kinged." Kings can move both forward and backward but, again, only diagonally. When you are kinged, a second checker is placed on top of the first.
- To move forward, one player can jump another player provided the diagonal space behind it is empty. In order to take an opponent's checker, a player must use the word on the checker in the sentence.
- In this adaptation, you must use the word written on your checker as you move it. For example, if your checker reads "frighten," a student might say, "Don't let the scary movie frighten you." The word can be used anywhere in the sentence, but it must be used accurately in meaning and part of speech.
- When a checker moves twice in a row, the player must generate another sentence with it.

Moving Forward

- Like Tower Tumble, Checkers has a ton of variations. There are endless cross-curricular possibilities, as Checkers might have content-area words on them. Just complete a unit on the environment? Select words—or have students select them—that relate to the topic and display them on checker pieces.

- I've also seen "Poetry Checkers" where students work with their partner to incorporate all of the words on the Checkers into a thematic poem. For instance, each checker piece might have a "winter-themed" word on it (snow, blizzard, mittens, etc.), and students write a poem incorporating the words in order of each checker.

 **Minute Mentor**

I adapted the Checkers idea from *Two-for-One Teaching: Connecting Instruction to Student Values* (Porosoff & Weinstein, 2020).

For more information, check out this Scholastic blog:

- https://www.scholastic.com/teachers/blog-posts/nancy-jang/17-18/five-games-for-centers

A TO Z ABOUT

END OF DAY

Materials Needed

- A to Z About graphic organizer (download available from the online companion website: resources.corwin.com/everyminutematters)

Quick Overview and Rationale

"Brain dumps," where you quickly brainstorm all the things that you know and remember about a particular topic, are particularly useful to cement learning. In A to Z About, students generate a word for each alphabetic letter about a topic they've just studied. The activity helps students identify and retain key concepts in an engaging manner.

Step-by-Step Directions

TEACHER MODELING

- On the SMART Board or butcher paper, replicate or project the A to Z About graphic organizer (see photo p. 103). Begin with a topic familiar to all students, and showcase how to generate words or short phrases that correspond to every letter of the alphabet. For instance, if the topic is insects, you might think aloud with "My job is to think of a word that relates to insects that starts with the letter *a*. I know that insects have antenna, so I'm going to write that down in my A box."

- Demonstrate how to brainstorm ideas for each letter of the alphabet. You might simply do a brain dump of all of the words and terms that you associate with a particular topic. Later on, you can place the list in the alphabetic letter boxes.

- Examples from other students also help students to understand their task. Focus their attention on how the idea is to generate essential words that are significant to the topic, rather than nonessential words.

STUDENT PRACTICE

- As students become more familiar with the activity, you might use the gradual release of responsibility to transfer ownership toward them. They might work in pairs before they are ready to work independently. You might encourage them to search in their books and related text sets for essential words.

Moving Forward

- For very young students or those with limited language, you might group letters together (e.g., A-B, C-D, W-X-Y-Z). This reduces the number of terms that students generate.

- Challenge students to explain why they've selected each word: what it means and why it is essential to the topic. This follow-up activity challenges students to be metacognitive about their selections and learning.

Minute Mentor

- Interested in activities related to retrieval practice? I highly recommend the resources on www .retrievalpractice.org as well as the book *Making It Stick: The Science of Successful Learning* (Brown, Roediger, & McDaniel (2014).

A Anti Raanta	B Blue line	C center	D Defence	E Eric Staal	F clargile flame's
GOAlie	Hiemet	ICe Hockey		Iceing	Jesper Fast
Keith Yandle	L tama bay lihgting			Marc Staal	N Rick Nash
Olla Schader's	Pitseurgh Peguens	Quick	Ranger	Stick	Toronto Mapel leafs
USa hockey	viktor Stalberg	Wirst shot	X	Yard sale	Zamboni

A to Z About Graphic Organizer

A	B	C	D	E	F
G	H	I			J
K	L			M	N
O	P	Q	R	S	T
U	V	W	X	Y	Z

Notes

STiCKY SORT

Link to Literacy

 Reading

 Writing

Materials Needed

- Sticky notes (10 per small group)
- Individual copies of a text
- Markers

Quick Overview and Rationale

Have you ever found yourself saying "Write a quick summary" as your students complete a book or a unit? Are you met by groans? Do your students struggle to summarize—focusing on the minutia while overlooking essential information? While summarization is a tried-but-true strategy, it is quite difficult for many students—as it forces them to distill the essential from the nonessential.

My answer to summarization comes from Ruth and Hallie Yopp (2007), who designed "Ten Important Words Plus." Here, students revisit a text and select its 10 most important words. My version is a slight modification of their ideas. In fact, I like this experience so much that I use it when I work with graduate students and in professional development workshops.

 ## Step-by-Step Directions

TEACHER MODELING

- At the conclusion of a unit of study or a nonfiction text, model selecting the 10 most important words that are essential to understand the topic or text. The following sentence starters might help jump-start your think aloud of selecting words:
  - » When I think of this topic, _____ is an essential word.
  - » I need to include the word _____ when I talk about…
  - » The word _____ is important to include when I think about …

STUDENT PRACTICE

- Give small groups of students a stack of 10 sticky notes. Have them spend approximately 6 to 8 minutes identifying the 10 key words or phrases from their text. Once they've selected their words, have them write them in large print on sticky notes (one word per sticky note).

- Next, give each group a section of the wall, whiteboard, or even a piece of poster board to serve as their backdrop. Their mission is to sort the sticky notes and arrange them into any shape. If they are sorting historical terms, their shape might be a timeline to indicate an order of events. If the words can be grouped into categories, _____. As they move the words into a shape or formation, students are making sense of how each word contributes to the essential information in the text or unit of study.

- You might encourage small groups to share their shapes and explain their thinking. I like to snap photos of their shapes and upload them to shared folders (like Google Classroom) and then allow kids to use these photos as a springboard to reflect in writing about the process. A prompt might be "Tell me about the words you selected and the shape you formed" or "Explain how these words or shapes helped you understand _____."

Moving Forward

- You might also reduce the number of target words to begin this process as the number of 10 might be too much.

- To provide additional support, provide the words for students. Because it's more challenging for students to select the words themselves, they can begin the sorting process with the teacher-selected words.

- Gradually decrease the number of teacher-supplied words while increasing the number of student-selected words.

Minute Mentor

I've modified this experience from Yopp and Yopp's (2007) "Ten Important Words Plus."

READiNG GRAFFiTi

END OF DAY

Materials Needed

- A portion of classroom wall, door, or bulletin board
- Butcher paper

Quick Overview and Rationale

As a reader, I have a notebook where I've copied down particularly powerful quotes from a book or a character. Reading Graffiti provides a visible space in the classroom for all readers to share quotes from their books that resonate with them. Originally presented in Donalyn Miller's (2013) *Reading in the Wild*, Reading Graffiti helps transform reading from an individual event into a social activity.

 ## Step-by-Step Directions

TEACHER MODELING

- Model the process of finding powerful quotes from a book that you are sharing in a whole-class read aloud. (*Fish in a Tree* [Hunt, 2015] and *Wonder* [Palacio, 2012] are great chapter books for Reading Graffiti; *Love* by Matt de la Peña (2018) is a fabulous picture book.)

- Introduce the Reading Graffiti wall as a place to write quotes from books that inspire us to be better people or to make our world a better place. Explain that these quotes might be spoken through the characters from our books. (See the photo below for a lovely example.)

- As you encounter a powerful quote, explain it, model writing it on the Reading Graffiti wall. The following questions are useful to think aloud as you model your selection: Why did the character say that? How does the quote apply to our lives? How is it powerful? Does the quote make sense out of context? In other words, if we only read that quote, would it make sense?

STUDENT PRACTICE

- To ensure that students understand the process, have them check in with you before writing their quotes on the Reading Graffiti wall. Use those questions to check in with and give each child permission to add their quote. As they read, students might jot their quotes down on a sticky note and hold them until you've got time to check in.

- At the conclusion of the day or at the end of a period of independent reading, encourage students to add quotes to the wall.

Moving Forward

- Use the Reading Graffiti wall as a conversation starter for reading conferences. When you meet with each child, have him explain the context of his quote and why he chose it.

- When the wall is covered, lead the class in voting on the most powerful quote.

Minute Mentor

Read more about this idea in Donalyn Miller's (2013) *Reading in the Wild*.

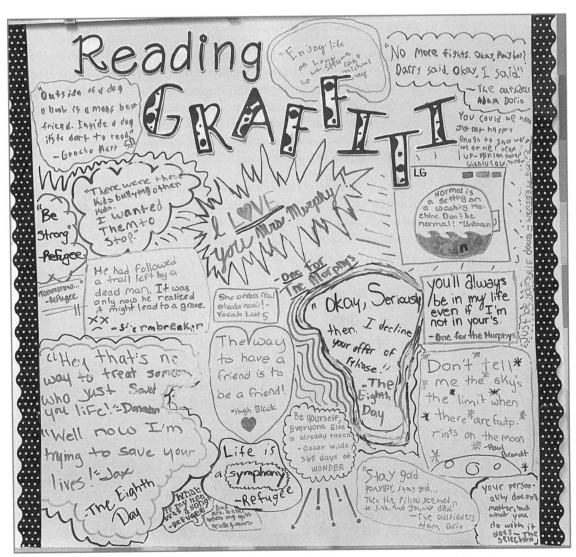

Fifth graders add important lines from their independent reading to the Classroom Graffiti wall.

Materials Needed

- Large sheets of sticky paper or butcher paper
- Markers

Quick Overview and Rationale

Do you include gallery walks as a classroom strategy designed to scaffold conversation? In a gallery walk, the teacher posts some kind of work or thinking and encourages students to circulate through the room, while responding and thinking. H. "Smokey" Daniels (2011) explains that the "fundamental process [of a gallery walk] involves hanging up various graphic and/or textual displays, and then having kids interact around them in a purposeful way, often leaving behind written comments as they go" (p. 115).

When one of my students posed, "Can I leave a quick drawing instead of a note?," my gallery walk became the Jot Lot. In my work with younger students and with students acquiring English, the modified Jot Lot became a powerful way for students to respond to texts—both narrative and informational—in a combination of words and pictures. Tammy McGregor (2018) calls this sketchnoting, a creative, individualized note-taking combination of linguistic and nonlinguistic representations.

A Jot Lot asks students to respond—in writing or illustrating—to questions posed on large pieces of paper. Armed with a marker, children circulate for a specified amount of time and respond to prompts atop the paper. Not only do students get up and moving but the Jot Lot is a great place to send students who finish work ahead of time.

 ## Step-by-Step Directions

TEACHER MODELING

- Select a topic for your Jot Lot, and write it at the top of a large piece of butcher paper. Choose a topic broad enough to elicit many responses; it might be a word, a book title, or a topic that you've covered in content-area instruction. Some of my favorite topics to start with are "Sports," "Holidays," and "Nature," because they are broad enough for students to have sufficient background knowledge.

- Think aloud as you talk through what comes to mind. When I used a Jot Lot in a fourth-grade classroom, we chose *Harry Potter* as our topic because we were sharing the book as a read aloud. I modeled by saying, "When I think of *Harry Potter*, there are many things that jump to mind that I could add to the Jot Lot. I could draw a lightning-shaped scar, or I could write the word *wizard*." Model adding a few key terms or sketches.

- As you model adding to the Jot Lot, practice using this sentence frame: "I am adding _____ to the Jot Lot because _____." This frame encourages students to explain and justify their decision.
- To begin the process, you might add to the Jot Lot at designated times, such as after finishing a chapter of each book.

STUDENT PRACTICE

- Explain to students that the Jot Lot will remain visible for a certain period and that they can add to it as time allows or as things come to mind.
- Also remind students that the Jot Lot is meant for quick sketches (no need for extended art projects) and a few words (where I disregard spelling and mechanics).

 **Moving Forward**

- Have students turn and talk to a partner about their contributions to the Jot Lot. Encourage them to explain how they selected their words or sketches to represent the topic at hand.
- You might also encourage students to add a Jot Lot page to their Reader's Notebook and use that page to jump-start your reading conferences (e.g., "Explain to me the words and sketches that you've added to your Jot Lot. What do they show and represent about your book?").

 **Minute Mentor**

For a thorough explanation of gallery walks, try this resource:

- Daniels, H. (2011). *Texts and lessons for content-area reading*. Portsmouth, NH: Heinemann.

For a thorough explanation of sketchnoting, try this book:

- McGregor, T. (2018). *Ink and ideas: Sketchnotes for engagement, comprehension, and thinking*. Portsmouth, NH: Heinemann.

WORDOODLE

Link to Literacy

 Reading

 Writing

END OF DAY

Materials Needed

- Vocabulary words that have recently been defined or introduced

Quick Overview and Rationale

When I was 7, I plowed through the Ramona series. A memory that still sticks with me is Ramona's illustration of her last name; she converted her capital Q into a doodle of a cat, complete with whiskers and ears. That image stuck with me as a young reader still mastering my letter formation; never again did I struggle to make my capital Q. (See photo p. 113.)

In hindsight, I recognize that Ramona made a Wordoodle (a word doodle), where an illustration that depicts the meaning of a vocabulary word. A tried and true way to reinforce vocabulary instruction is to illustrate or sketch words, a practice particularly useful to English language learners. A Wordoodle extends this idea, challenging the reader to cleverly integrate the letters of the word into her illustration. In fact, so popular is this approach that it's been adopted by vocabulary programs like Mrs. Wordsmith.

 ## Step-by-Step Directions

TEACHER MODELING

- Model the process of writing out a vocabulary word and thinking through how you'd illustrate it. I used the example of the word *frost*, which stemmed from my read aloud of Chris Van Allsburg's (1986) *The Stranger*. In this student sample shown on page 113, the child has turned the letters into icicles. In another example (p. 113), a student has drawn plants growing out of the word *seed*.

- As you encounter words that lend themselves to Wordoodles, lead a brainstorm in how you might illustrate the word—being sure to incorporate the actual letters into the illustration.

STUDENT PRACTICE

- Transfer responsibility to students by selecting words for them to convert into a Wordoodle.

- Eventually, students might be ready to choose their own words.

 ## Moving Forward

- To extend this activity, you might use Wordoodles as a quick check for students' vocabulary knowledge or as an activity to review vocabulary prior to an assessment. For instance, students might partner up and explain their Wordoodles to each other.

- Encourage students to keep Wordoodles in their Reader's Notebooks or to add them to a class word wall.

Minute Mentor

For more information on the power of doodling to improve vocabulary, check out these resources:

- https://learning.blogs.nytimes.com/2015/09/24/skills-and-strategies-doodling-sketching-and-mind-mapping-as-learning-tools

- Claggett, F. (1992). *Drawing your own conclusions: Graphic strategies for reading, writing and thinking.* Portsmouth, NH: Heinemann.

- Simmons, E. (2002). Visualizing vocabulary. *The Quarterly, 24.*

- Baumann, J. F., Edwards, E. C., Boland, E., Olejnik, S., & Kame'enui, E. (2003). Vocabulary tricks: Effects of instruction in morphology and context on fifth grade students' ability to derive and infer word meanings. *American Educational Research Journal, 40,* 447–494.

This creative student sketches seedlings to depict the word *seed* and icicles for *frost.*

WORDO

Link to Literacy

 Reading

 Writing

Materials Needed

- Individual copies of Wordo boards (download available from the online companion website: resources.corwin.com/everyminutematters)

- Bingo daubers (not necessary but awfully fun!)

Quick Overview and Rationale

Guilty confession: In my first year of teaching, every Friday was a spelling test. Years later, I can hear the collective groan of my students echoing in my memory. While the problem wasn't my need for some sort of assessment, it was the monotony of the particular assessment that I chose. If only I had known about Wordo.

Wordo is an adaptation of the perennial favorite bingo. I love Wordo because it turns an assessment immediately into a game and reinforces spelling and vocabulary. Anytime you need to assess word study or spelling, turn your students' groans into cheers with Wordo!

 ## Step-by-Step Directions

TEACHER MODELING

- At the culmination of a spelling or word study unit, distribute blank Wordo boards.

- Conduct the dictation as normal; in other words, call out the word, use it in a sentence, and repeat the word. Students can write the target word in any box of their choice. In other words, every student's board will look different (just as every bingo board looks different).

- Call out all the word study or spelling words until their boards are filled.

- Now you're ready to play Wordo, but rather than saying the word itself, give clues around the word. For example, on the board below, if I were giving a clue for the word *toast*, I might give this clue: "For breakfast, I had eggs and ____."

- For increased engagement, vary your clues as much as possible. For instance, with the word *knock*, I might state "The sound you hear..." and then I might rap my knuckles on the desk.

- When a student has a row, column, or diagonal line connected, he calls out "Wordo!" The winner then has to correctly spell aloud all of their words.

 **Moving Forward**

- Differentiate your clues according to your students' levels and background knowledge. For instance, if I'm aiming for the word *toad* and I know my students have covered this content in science, I might say, "This is an amphibian." Or I might use the words *synonym* or *antonym* in my clues, as in "This word is a synonym for jacket" to aim for the target word *coat*.

- Collect their Wordo boards and assess them as you'd do with a regular spelling or word study test.

- Encourage kids to glue their Wordo boards into their Reader's Notebooks so that they become references for future spelling. This way rather than the constant "How do you spell?" you can encourage them to search for it in their Reader's Notebook.

 **Minute Mentor**

For more innovative ideas on incorporating games into word study, check out two of my favorite resources:

- Bear, D., Invernizzi, M., Templeton, S., & Johnston, F. (2015). *Words their way: Word study for phonics, vocabulary, and spelling* (6th ed.) New York, NY: Pearson.

- Koutrakos, P. (2019). *Word study that sticks: Best practices K–6.* Thousand Oaks, CA: Corwin.

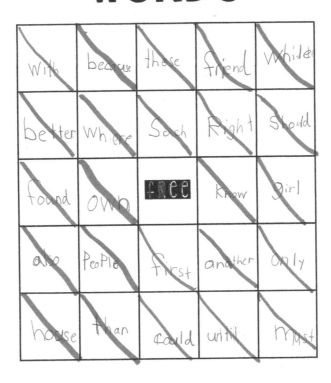

Wordo Board

WORDO

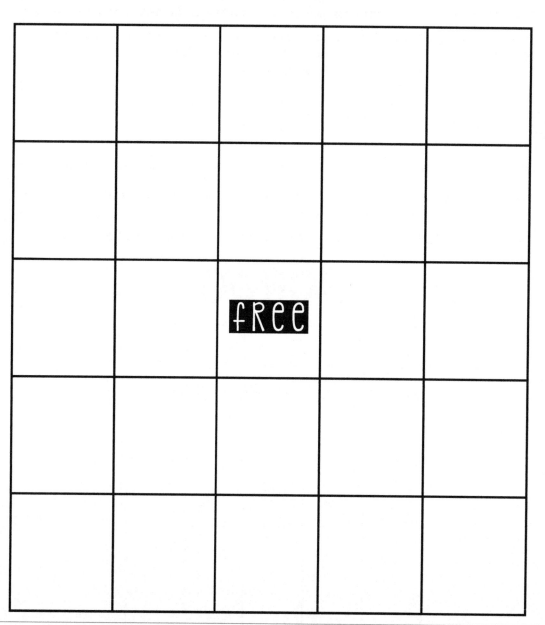

Notes

CHARACTER CARDS

Writing

END OF DAY

Materials Needed

- General art supplies
- Blank Character Card template (download available from the online companion website: resources.corwin.com/everyminutematters)

Quick Overview and Rationale

My grandmother confiscated my father's baseball cards (he swears he once owned a Mickey Mantle rookie card, now worth approximately $1 million). My third-grade teacher confiscated my Garbage Pail Kids (remember those horrible 1980s relics?). As a sixth-grade teacher, I confiscated my students' Pokemon cards. Whatever the era and whatever the subject, kids love collecting and swapping trading cards. Rather than banishing them from school, how about we incorporate them in a creative way? I use Character Cards as a way to represent key historical figures or book characters.

 ## Step-by-Step Directions

TEACHER MODELING

- Project a handful of sports cards for students to see. Choose a sampling of sports and athletes that represent the makeup and interest of your students. Lead a conversation encouraging students to brainstorm on the following:
  - » What do you notice about these cards?
  - » What information do we find on these cards?
  - » What is the purpose of these cards?
  - » How might we make our own cards for the people and characters we've been studying?

- Choose one character or historical figure to model. Use the Character Card template to think aloud about the appearance and features of your character. One first grader (see p. 119) drew a Character Card of Mr. Magee from the picture book *Down to the Sea With Mr. Magee* (Van Dusen, 2000).

STUDENT PRACTICE

- After you've completed a Character Card, distribute the templates. Encourage students to add them to their Reader's Notebooks and add to them as they encounter new information about their characters.

 **Moving
Forward**

- Create time for students to share their Character Cards with their classmates, and encourage them to add engaging statistics. Whereas a baseball player's card lists their batting average, Ron Weasley's Character Card might list spiders as his "greatest fear."

- Character Cards are also fun ways to represent historical figures in content-area classrooms. For example, when studying the American Revolution, students might work in small groups to create Character Cards for Paul Revere or Benjamin Franklin. You might also create Character Cards when you engage in author studies—better yet, upload the Character Cards and send them to the author!

 **Minute
Mentor**

I've adapted this idea from some suggested in this book:

- Rollins, Q. (2016). *Play like a pirate: Engage students with toys, games, and comics.* San Diego, CA: Dave Burgess Consulting.

Character Card Template

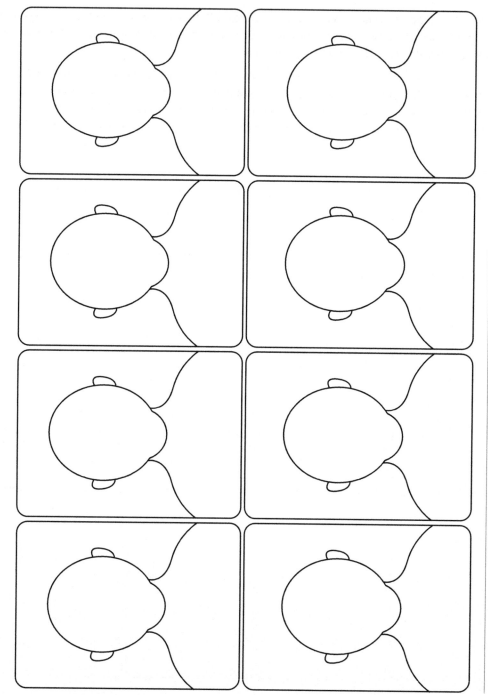

Notes

_____

_____

_____

_____

_____

_____

_____

_____

_____

_____

_____

_____

CATEGORIES

Link to Literacy

Writing

Materials Needed

- Alphabet spinner (make your own with the download available from the online companion website: resources.corwin.com/everyminutematters, or use this free electronic one https://wheeldecide.com/wheels/board -games/scattegories-spinner

- Category list (in the appendix)

- Individual copies of Categories card (download available from the online companion website: resources.corwin.com/everyminutematters)

Quick Overview and Rationale

I love word games! Admittedly I don't love playing word games with my closest friend, who has memorized every esoteric two-letter word that earns big points in Scrabble. (He destroyed me in a recent game, racking up big points for the words *oe, ai, jo, mu, xi, qi,* and *aa.*) Among my favorite games is Scattergories, which challenges players to generate as many words beginning with a particular letter that match the provided category. How many breakfast foods starting with the letter *B* can you think of? What about animals starting with the letter *R*? You've just played Scattergories, a wordplay game that builds speed and awards students for creativity. Players score points by uniquely naming objects within a set of categories, given an initial letter, within a time limit. Here's how to play Categories in your classroom.

 ## Step-by-Step Directions

TEACHER MODELING

- Choose a broad category like "Girl Names," "Sports," or "Things You Wear." It's also useful for children to see two adults playing against each other, so grab your aide, a neighbor, or a parent volunteer.

- Use the alphabet spinner (paper copy or electronic) to determine which letter to begin with.

- Think aloud as you talk through brainstorming in a 2-minute time period. For example, if the category is "Girl Names" and your letter is *J*, you could talk through "Jennifer, Janice, Jen, Jasmine, Jackie, Jade, and so on." Remind students that spelling does not count.

- All players stop writing when the timer is finished. Following the list, each player, in turn, reads their answer for each category. Players score zero points for an answer that duplicates another answer in that round and one point for an answer no other player has given.

- If for some reason a player thinks someone's answer does not fit the category (for instance, "knuckle" for the category "Types of Sandwich"), a player may challenge that answer. When challenged, all players vote on the validity of that answer. If the vote is a tie, the vote of the player who is being challenged is thrown out.

Moving Forward

- This can be played in teams or as individuals.
- Use tablets to allow students to record, then listen to their brainstorm, and finally write the list.
- Vary the rules so that students only earn points for words that are unique to their lists; this encourages students to think creatively and expand their vocabularies.
- Have one team think of a category and another team pick a letter. Set the timer, and see which team can come up with the most answers.
- For English language learners, encourage them to generate lists in their native languages.
- Use this as a review activity at the end of a unit or in preparation for a test. So, at the end of a social studies unit, you might provide "American Revolution" as the category and then choose a letter.
- For additional support, have children work in partners to brainstorm together before having them work individually.
- Encourage students to come up with their own categories.
- For even more support, allow children to use two letters; so you might have them name "Foods That Start With *B* and *S*." As you increase the number of letters, you avoid children getting stuck.
- Integrate Categories into content-area instruction. For instance, after a science unit, can your students do a Categories card for "Amphibians"? How about a card in social studies for "Native Americans"?

Minute Mentor

Still not convinced of the academic benefits of games in the classroom? Check out these resources for further proof on how games increase vocabulary, facilitate critical thinking, and motivate students:

- Blachowicz, C. L. (2004). *Keep the "fun" in fundamental: Encouraging word awareness and incidental word learning in the classroom through word play.* New York, NY: Guilford Press.
- Hinebaugh, J. P. (2009) *A board game education: Building skills for academic success.* New York, NY: Rowman & Littlefield.

Categories Card

The letter is:	The letter is:
The category is:	The category is:
Answers:	Answers:

The letter is:	The letter is:
The category is:	The category is:
Answers:	Answers:

Notes

CHARACTER CHATS

Link to Literacy

Writing

Materials Needed

- Age-appropriate writing paper or writing journals
- Online timer to help countdown time (I like using the Google Timer on my SMART Board)

Quick Overview and Rationale

What would Willy Wonka say to Albus Dumbledore if they hypothetically could meet? What would Elephant and Piggy say if they ever met the Cat in the Hat? How about the Wimpy Kid (Greg Heffler) chat with Big Nate? Imagine the creative and engaging writing that children might produce as a result of Character Chats. I first began using Character Chats as a way for my students to truly understand a character's point of view. In a Character Chat, kids take the first-person perspective of a particular character and write a letter to another character. There are two ways to do Character Chats: (1) characters within a book writing to each other and (2) characters from across different books writing to each other.

 ## Step-by-Step Directions

TEACHER MODELING

- Model drafting a Character Chat after a shared read aloud. I love using Pam Muñoz Ryan's (1999) *Amelia and Eleanor Go for a Ride* as my mentor text, since it tells of the little known friendship between Amelia Earhart and Eleanor Roosevelt.

- After sharing the book with students, I think aloud while imaging writing a letter from Eleanor Roosevelt to Amelia Earhart. I invite students to help me brainstorm a subsequent letter from Amelia back to Eleanor.

STUDENT PRACTICE

- To jump-start their writing, begin with these questions:
  - » If these two characters could talk or write letters to each other, what might they say?
  - » What questions might they ask one another?
  - » What do they have in common?

Moving Forward

- It is less complex to do Character Chats within a book than to apply the notion across books. I usually begin here.

- I like to follow up the Character Chat writing with conversations between the writing partners. The following questions might jump-start conversations:
  » Was there anything that your partner wrote that surprised you?
  » Did your characters have more agreements or disagreements? Similarities or differences?
  » If the characters continued to write, where might their conversation go next?

Minute Mentor

Character chats are really just a modification on the ever-popular dialogue journals, which facilitate written conversation between teachers and students. This article explains how and why to incorporate dialogue journals into the classroom:

- Denne-Bolton, S. (2003). The dialogue journal: A tool for building better writers. *English Teaching Forum, 13*, 1–13.

BLACKOUT POETRY

Link to Literacy

Writing

Materials Needed

- Individual copies of photocopied pages of text

Quick Overview and Rationale

Do your students struggle to get started writing poetry? Let's face it, to many students, poetry writing is an intimidating process. When my former students began poetry writing, I'd often hear, "I don't know how to get started!" But what if students could make original poetry by borrowing words from a page? That's the beauty of Blackout Poetry. Texas-based writer Austin Kleon is often given credit for creating Blackout Poetry, but many teachers may have previously known them as "found poetry."

 ### Step-by-Step Directions

TEACHER MODELING

- Select a student-friendly short text to use for modeling. My favorite sources are short articles from *Time for Kids* or other similar magazines.

- Think aloud as you skim the text for appealing words. This is the Brainstorming Round, where you overidentify words and phrases. Circle those words and/or phrases. These sentence starters might be useful as you think aloud.
  - » I'm selecting the word or phrase _____ because _____.
  - » The word or phrase _____ jumps out at me because _____.

- Jot down the words that you've circled, and read the list aloud.

- Now model the Revision Round by crossing out any words that you decide not to use. Think aloud with these sentence starters so that students see your process:
  - » I'm eliminating the word _____ because _____.
  - » On second thought, I don't need this word _____.
  - » One word that isn't really necessary in this list is _____.

- Once you've finalized your list of words, go back through the text and highlight them so they are visible. Draw a box around them, or use a highlighter so the words jump off of the page.

- Copy down your poem, and read aloud to the class.

- Encourage conversations that allow students to react to your poem. These sentence starters might be useful:

  - » My favorite part of the poem is...
  - » When I listened to the poem, I felt...
  - » This process of writing Blackout Poetry helped me by...

STUDENT PRACTICE

- Begin by giving students a concrete number of words or phrases. For instance, you might say, "In the Brainstorming Round, you should circle at least 10 words or phrases. In the Revision Round, reduce your number to 7 words."

Moving Forward

- Some students enjoy actually blacking out the remaining unused portions of the text. They can use a marker or pen to black out everything that is not a word in their poem. Additionally, they can add a sketch to their poem.

- Blackout Poetry is particularly useful for content-based texts in social studies and science.

- Blackout Poetry can serve as a fantastic text to encourage fluency practice, as students read and reread their original works to perform.

Minute Mentor

Check out some fabulous blogs that further explain the whys and hows of Blackout Poetry. There's even a TED Talk by writer Austin Kleon!

- http://www.nowsparkcreativity.com/2018/10/the-easy-guide-to-blackout-poetry.html
- https://www.powerpoetry.org/actions/5-tips-creating-blackout-poetry
- https://ncte.org/blog/2019/04/blackout-poetry

Sample Text for Blackout Poetry (excerpt from Gail Gibbons's [2006]*Owls*)

Excerpt from *Owls* by Gail Gibbons

On silent wings a bird swoops down in the moonlight. The bird is an owl. Using its powerful claws, it grabs a field mouse. Owls are raptors.

Raptors are birds of prey, meaning they are hunters that eat meat. They grab their prey with claws, called talons, that are very sharp.

Most owls have the same basic characteristics. The male is usually a little smaller than the female. The eyes of an owl cannot move in their eye sockets to watch for prey. Instead, owls have flexible necks that can twist almost completely around. They can even turn their heads upside down.

Most owls hunt at night. Day or night, they can see much better than people. Owls have very large eyes. Owls can change the focus of their eyes very rapidly and see great distances. At night the pupils of their eyes get big. This allows more light to enter into their eyes, giving them unusually good vision in the dark.

Most owls rely on their keen hearing for hunting rather than their excellent vision. Their ears are hidden behind their facial disk feathers. These disks act like dish antennas to funnel sound to their ears.

Owls are constantly turning their heads to hear better.

An owl attacks its prey silently. When flying,

it can move its wings without making a sound.

Silence....

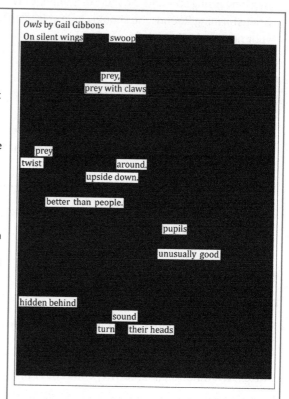

Available for download at **resources.corwin.com/everyminutematters**

APPENDIX

RECOMMENDED SUPPLIES

Supply	Ideas to Try
Alphabet bean bags	Have students in a circle pass the bean bag to their neighbor on the left. Before passing, they must name the letter and make its sound. Have several bean bags going at the same time for fun and speed. This can be added to Human Hungry Hippos and Lining Up With Literacy.
Fluency phones	Encourage students to reread and whisper into the phones, as the shape of fluency phones provides automatic auditory feedback.
Question dice	Each side has a different questioning stem; these serve as a great springboard for "I Wonder" Writing and the Parking Lot.
Classroom set of whiteboards	Use individual whiteboards as a quick check for understanding. In Hink Pinks, students might write their answer and hold it above their heads.
Alphabet dice or word family dice	Have students roll the dice to practice the sounds associated with each letter. Or have them roll the dice and write the letter and its capital, lowercase, or cursive version for handwriting practice. Have students use word family dice to practice blending onsets and rhymes.
Pool noodles	Help students with blending activities by slicing pool noodles into 2- to 3-inch slices. Write a letter on each (use one color for vowels and another for consonants). Thread a wooden dowel through the center, and you've got a great way to have students work on blending.
Craft sticks	Write vocabulary words on them for the Vocabulary Vase activity.
Easter eggs	Similar to the pool noodles from above, use a marker to write word families on the right portion of the egg and beginning sounds on the left side of the egg. Students twist the egg to practice blending word families.
Inflatable beach ball	Encourage conversation as you toss the ball around the room. At the start of the school year, your beach ball might have student names on it. Toss the ball, and use this as a way to learn everyone's name.
Voice changer	Kids get a kick out of rereading familiar text when their voice sounds like a robot or a mouse!
Kinetic sand	This is great to use for Letter Formation exercises.

(Continued)

(Continued)

Supply	Ideas to Try
Wax craft sticks (e.g., Wikki Stix)	Have students mold these flexible plastic sticks into letters, or use them to build sight words.
Finger lights	Encourage finger point reading, or use them for fun to have students point to words that they've selected for Blackout Poetry.
Magnetic poetry	There are endless possibilities to generate found poetry with the multiple versions of magnetic poetry that are now commercially available.

WORD-BASED GAMES THAT I LOVE

- Zingo Word Builder
- Zingo Sight Words
- See-It? Slam-It!
- Chain Letters
- Boggle Jr.
- Bananagrams
- Word-a-Round
- Tell Me a Story (Eeboo)
- Spot It
- Word Shout (Playmonster)
- Rory's Story Cubes (Gamewright)
- Super Genius Alphabet (Blue Orange)
- Super Genius Reading 2
- The Pretty Darn Quick Word Game (Gamewright)
- Taboo
- Twizmo
- Kabam
- Sight Word Splat
- Alphabet Bingo (Peaceable Kingdom)
- Turnspell (Mattel)
- Quiddler Jr. (Set Enterprises)
- WordSpiel (Set Enterprises)

QUICK IDEAS

Some of the best ideas don't need a lot of explanation, just a brief reminder. Here are some of my favorite literacy-based activities that are easy and engaging:

- Sight Word Splat: Put sight word cards on the floor, and have students use a fly swatter to catch the words, like a frog catches flies with its tongue. Students must read the words aloud.

- Roll and Read: Make your own dice on two colors of card stock using the template in the appendix. One color will have blends and digraphs written on each side of the cube; the other color will have word families. Students roll the dice and read the words, and then they use them in a sentence (silly sentences are fine!)

- Buy a plastic bowling set at the dollar store, and tape sight words onto the pins. When students bowl, they have to read and use words from the knocked-down pins.

- For younger kids, glue two toilet paper tubes together and make "reading binoculars." Have them use their new binoculars to spot environmental print and read word walls.

- Write letters on plastic building blocks (e.g., Legos or Duplos) and place in a bin. When students finish a book, have them build a tower spelling the book title out of Legos. Proudly display your towers to document your reading successes.

- Make word chains: similar to the paper chains used for holiday decorations, have students write rhyming word families on each link of the chain.

- Take paint samples from the hardware store, cut out a window, and create word family books. Do the same with plastic Easter eggs and pool noodles.

SUGGESTED CATEGORIES

Genres of books	Hobbies	Things that start with the letter M
Things with pockets	Professions	Colors
Ways to exercise	Colleges	Things that start with the letter Q
Things that start with the letter Z	Things that are orange jewelry	Things that use batteries
Things that are alive	Things that start with the letter O	Types of breakfast cereal
Things that are green	Things that use electricity	Nicknames
Famous musicians	Things that fly	Items found in a kitchen
Jewelry	School supplies	Things you can see with a microscope
Car parts	Famous men	Tools
Things that start with the letter T	Items found in a purse	Song titles
Languages	Fruits and vegetables	Sports teams
Sports	Companies	Books
Things you can see from an airplane window	Things that are black	Things that spin
Things that start with the letter P	Things you wear on your head	Things with screens
Things that are yellow	Emotions	Things that float
Types of wood	Creatures that live in the ocean	Farm animals
School subjects	Things that start with the letter N	Things found in outer space
Reptiles	Clothing stores	States in the United States of America
Travel destinations	Mammals	Ways to cook something
Things with wheels	Clothing	Ways to get from one place to another
Heroes	Models of cars	Types of sandwiches
Things you plug in	Famous historical figures	Things made of glass
Types of birds	Things made of wood	Famous athletes
Genres of movies	Things you can turn on and off	Things made of fabric
Terms of endearment	Famous actors	Things that are gray
Things that are white	Items found in a bathroom	Condiments
Wild animals	Fictional characters	Things with buttons
Things that are blue	College majors	Things that start with the letter J
Board games	Things in a mall	Things that are pink
Junk food	Things that sink	Things found under a bed
Fast food	Countries	Things that are purple

Things made of metal	Female names	Male names
Things found on a map	Things that start with the letter A	Things at the beach
Names for a pet dog	Recipes	Genres of music
Road signs	Vehicles	Things that are red
Things you hang on a wall	Names in the Bible	Things that grow
Fads	Restaurants	

References

Allen, J. (2000). *Yellow brick road: Shared and guided paths to independent reading.* Portsmouth, NH: Stenhouse.

Bates, C., & Morgan, D. (2018). Addressing the barriers of time. *The Reading Teacher, 72,* 131–134. Retrieved from https://doi .org/10.1002/trtr.1716

Baumann, J. F., Edwards, E. C., Boland, E., Olejnik, S., & Kame'enui, E. (2003). Vocabulary tricks: Effects of instruction in morphology and context on fifth grade students' ability to derive and infer word meanings. *American Educational Research Journal, 40,* 447–494.

Bear, D., Invernizzi, M., Templeton, S., & Johnston, F. (2015). *Words their way: Word study for phonics, vocabulary, and spelling* (6th ed.) New York, NY: Pearson.

Beck, I., McKeown, M., & Kucan, L. (2013). *Bringing words to life: Robust vocabulary instruction.* New York, NY: Guilford Press.

Blachowicz, C. (2004). *Keep the "fun" in fundamental: Encouraging word awareness and incidental word learning in the classroom through word play.* New York, NY: Guilford Press.

Blevins, W. (2017). *A fresh look at phonics: Common causes of failure and 7 ingredients for success.* Thousand Oaks, CA: Corwin.

Brinkerhoff, E., & Roehrig, A. (2014). *No more sharpening pencils during work time and other time wasters.* Portsmouth, NH: Heinemann.

Brent, R., & Anderson, P. (1992). Developing children's classroom listening strategies. *The Reading Teacher, 47,* 122–126.

Brewer, P. (2003). *You must be joking!: Cool jokes, plus 17 ½ tips for remembering, telling, and making up your own jokes.* Battle Creek, MI: Cricket.

Brown, P., Roediger, H., & McDaniel, M. (2014). *Making it stick: The science of successful learning.* Cambridge, MA: Belknap Press.

Burkhalter, N. (1995). Vygotsky-based curriculum for teaching persuasive writing in the elementary grades. *Language Arts, 72,* 192–199.

Cartwright, K. (2015). *Executive skills and reading comprehension: A guide for educators.* New York, NY: Guilford Press.

Claggett, F. (1992). *Drawing your own conclusions: Graphic strategies for reading, writing and thinking.* Portsmouth, NH: Heinemann.

Cobb, C., & Blachowicz, C. (2014). *No more "look up the list" vocabulary instruction.* Portsmouth, NH: Heinemann.

Codding, R. S., & Smyth, C. A. (2008). Using performance feedback to decrease classroom transition time and examine collateral effects on academic engagement. *Journal of Educational & Psychological Consultation, 18,* 325–345.

Dahl, M. (2002). *The everything kids' joke book: Side-splitting, rib-tickling fun!* Cincinnati, OH: Adams Media.

Daniels, H. (2011). *Texts and lessons for content-area reading.* Portsmouth, NH: Heinemann.

Daniels, H. (2017). *The curious classroom: 10 structures for teaching with student-directed inquiry.* Portsmouth, NH: Heinemann.

Day, S. L., Connor, C. M., & McClelland, M. M. (2015). Children's behavioral regulation and literacy: The impact of the first-grade classroom environment. *Journal of School Psychology, 53,* 409–428.

de la Peña, M. (2018). *Love.* New York, NY: G. P. Putnam's Sons.

Denne-Bolton, S. (2003). The dialogue journal: A tool for building better writers. *English Teaching Forum, 13,* 1–13.

Diestefano, D., & Ness, M. (2018). Using hand symbols to scaffold student-generated questions in kindergarten classrooms. *Young Children, 73,* 22–28.

Duke, N. K., Cervetti, G. N., & Wise, C. N. (2018). Learning from exemplary teachers of literacy. *The Reading Teacher, 71,* 395–400. doi:10.1002/trtr.1654

Fieser, J. (1999). Variations on Go Fish: Making the most of an old game for the language classroom. *The Language Teacher, 23.*

Fisher, D. (2009). The use of instructional time in the typical high school classroom. *The Educational Forum, 73,* 168–176.

Fountas, I., & Pinnell, G. S. (2018). *The literacy quick guide: A reference tool for responsive literacy teaching.* Portsmouth, NH: Heinemann.

Frazier, B. N., Gelman, S. A., & Wellman, H. M. (2009). Preschoolers search for explanatory information within adult–child conversation. *Child Development, 80,* 1592–1611. doi:10.1111/j.1467-8624.2009.01356.x

Ganske, K. (2017). Lesson closure: An important piece of the student learning puzzle. *The Reading Teacher, 71,* 95–100. doi:10.1002/trtr.1587

Gerovasiliou, F., & Zafiri, M. (2017). Adapting board games to stimulate motivation in vocabulary learning in six year old learners—A case study. *Journal of Studies in Education, 7.*

Gibbons, G. (2006). *Owls.* New York, NY: Holiday House.

Harmin, M., & Toth, M. (2006). *Inspiring active learning: A complete handbook for today's teachers.* Washington, DC: Association for Supervision & Curriculum Development.

Harvey, S., & Ward, A. (2017). *From striving to thriving: How to grow confident, capable readers.* New York, NY: Scholastic

Hinebaugh, J. P. (2009). *A board game education: Building skills for academic success.* New York, NY: Rowman & Littlefield.

Horsfall, J. (2003). *Kids' silliest jokes.* New York, NY: Sterling.

Hunt, L. M. (2015). *Fish in a tree.* New York, NY: Puffin Books.

International Literacy Association. (2018). *The power and promise of read aloud and independent reading.* [Literacy Leadership Institute]. Newark, DE: Author.

International Literacy Association. (2019). *Teaching and assessing spelling* [Literacy leadership brief]. Newark, DE: Author.

Jago, C. (2018). *The book in question: Why and how reading is in crisis.* Portsmouth, NH: Heinemann.

Jensen, E. (2005). *Teaching with the brain in mind.* Alexandria, VA: Association for Supervision and Curriculum Development.

Kelly, L., Ogden, M., & Moses, L. (2019). Speaking and listening in the primary grades. *Young Children, 74.*

Koutrakos, P. (2019). *Word study that sticks: Best practices K–6.* Thousand Oaks, CA: Corwin.

Lia, D. (2014). After 100 years, have we come full circle in lesson design? *Illinois Schools Journal, 94,* 7–24.

Mages, W. (2018). The effect of drama on language, perspective-taking, and imagination. *Early Childhood Research Quarterly, 45,* 224–237.

McGregor, T. (2018). *Ink and ideas: Sketchnotes for engagement, comprehension, and thinking.* Portsmouth, NH: Heinemann.

Miller, D. (2009). *The book whisperer: Awakening the inner reader in every child.* San Francisco, CA: Jossey-Bass.

Miller, D. (2013). *Reading in the wild: The book whisperer's keys to cultivating lifelong reading habits.* San Francisco, CA: Jossey-Bass.

Miller, D., & Moss, B. (2011). *No more independent reading without support.* Portsmouth, NH: Heinemann.

Miller, D., & Sharp, C. (2018). *Game changer! Book access for all kids.* New York, NY: Scholastic.

Morton, B., & Dalton, B. (2007). *Changes in instructional hours in four subjects by public school teachers of grades 1 through 4.* Washington, DC: US Department of Education, National Center for Education Statistics.

Mulligan, T., & Landrigan, C. (2018). *It's all about the books: How to create bookrooms and classroom libraries that inspire readers.* Portsmouth, NH: Heinemann.

Muñoz Ryan, P. (1999). *Amelia and Eleanor go for a ride.* New York, NY: Scholastic Press.

Ness, M. (2009). Laughing through rereadings: Using joke books to build fluency. *The Reading Teacher, 62,* 691–694.

Ness, M. (2011). Explicit reading comprehension instruction in elementary classrooms: Teacher use of reading comprehension strategies. *Journal of Research in Childhood Education, 25,* 1–20. doi:10.1080/02568543.2010.531076

Ness, M. (2013). Unpark those questions. *Educational Leadership, 71,* 74–76.

Ness, M. (2014). Moving student-generated questions out of the parking lot. *The Reading Teacher, 67,* 369–373.

Ness, M. (2015). *The question is the answer: Supporting student-generated queries in elementary classrooms.* Landover, MD: Rowman & Littlefield.

Ness, M. (2016). Reading comprehension strategies in secondary content-area classrooms: Teacher use of and attitudes toward reading comprehension instruction. *Reading Horizons, 49.* Retrieved from https://scholarworks.wmich.edu/reading_horizons/vol49/iss2/5

Ness, M. (2017). "Is that what I really sound like?": Using iPads for fluency practice. *The Reading Teacher, 70,* 611–615. doi:10.1002/trtr.1554

Palacio, R. J. (2012). *Wonder.* New York, NY: Alfred A. Knopf.

Palmer, J., & Invernizzi, M. (2014). *No more phonics and spelling worksheets.* Portsmouth, NH: Heinemann.

Pollock, J. E. (2007). *Improving student learning one teacher at a time.* Alexandria, VA: Association for Supervision and Curriculum Development.

Porosoff, L., & Weinstein, J. (2020). *Two-for-one teaching: Connecting instruction to student values.* Bloomington, IN: Solution Tree Press.

Rasinski, T., & Smith, M. C. (2018). *The megabook of fluency.* New York, NY: Scholastic.

Rawlins, A., & Invernizzi, M. (2018). Reconceptualizing sight words: Building an early reading vocabulary. *The Reading Teacher, 72,* 711–719.

Ripp, P. (2017). *Passionate readers: The art of reaching and engaging every child.* New York, NY: Routledge.

Rollins, Q. (2016). *Play like a pirate: Engage students with toys, games, and comics.* San Diego, CA: Dave Burgess Consulting.

Scholastic. (2018). *Kids and family reading report* (7th ed.). New York, NY: Author.

Simmons, E. (2002). Visualizing vocabulary. *The Quarterly, 24.*

Smith, B. A. (1998). *It's about time: Opportunities to learn in Chicago's elementary public schools.* Chicago, IL: Consortium on Chicago School Research.

Smith, B. A. (2000). Quantity matters: Annual instruction time in an urban school system. *Educational Administration Quarterly, 36,* 652–682.

Stanovich, K. E. (1986). Matthew effects in reading: Some consequences of individual differences in the acquisition of literacy. *Reading Research Quarterly, 21,* 360–407.

Sunny Panda. (2019). *Would you rather book for kids: The book of silly scenarios, challenging choices, and hilarious situations the whole family will love (game gift book ideas).* Online: Author.

Telegraph Staff. (2013, March 28). Mothers asked nearly 300 questions a day, study finds. *The Telegraph.* Retrieved from http://www.telegraph.co.uk/news/uknews/9959026/Mothers-asked-nearly-300-questions-a-day-study-finds.html

Terban, M. (2007). *Eight ate: A feast of homonym riddles.* New York, NY: Sandpiper.

Van Allsburg, C. (1986). *The stranger.* New York, NY: Houghton Mifflin.

Vanderkam, L. (2010). *168 hours: You have more time than you think.* New York, NY: Portfolio.

Van Dusen, C. W. (2000). *Down to the sea with Mr. Magee.* San Francisco, CA: Chronicle Books.

Vander Hart, N., Fitzpatrick, P., & Cortesa, C. (2010). In-depth analysis of handwriting curriculum and instruction in four kindergarten classrooms. *Reading and Writing, 23,* 673–699.

Weakland, M. (2017). *Super spellers: Seven steps to transform your spelling instruction.* Portsmouth, NH: Stenhouse.

Weitzman, I. (2006). *Jokelopedia: The biggest, best, silliest, dumbest joke book ever.* New York, NY: Workman.

Wolf, P., & Supon, V. (1994). Winning through student participation in lesson closure. Retrieved from ERIC database. (ED368694)

Wollman-Bonilla, J. (2000). *Family message journals: Teaching writing through family involvement.* Urbana, IL: National Council of Teachers of English.

Yopp, R., & Yopp, H. (2007). Ten important words plus: A strategy for building word knowledge. *The Reading Teacher, 61,* 157–160. doi:10.1598/RT.61.2

Yopp, H., & Yopp, R. (2009). Phonological awareness is child's play. *Young Children,* pp. 12–21.

INDEX

Because...
ALL TEACHERS ARE LEADERS

MOLLY NESS

Molly's three-step planning process will help you create dynamic lessons that focus on the five most important think aloud strategies.

DOUGLAS FISHER, NANCY FREY, AND NANCY AKHAVAN

Evidence-based approaches ensure that the teachers have all they need to achieve balance in their literacy classrooms across a wide range of critical skills.

GRETCHEN BERNABEI, KAYLA SHOOK, AND JAYNE HOVER

In 53 lessons centered around classic nursery rhymes, this groundbreaking book offers a straightforward framework for guiding young children in their earliest writing efforts.

WILEY BLEVINS

Foremost phonics expert Wiley Blevins explains the 7 ingredients that lead to the greatest student gains. This resource includes common pitfalls, lessons, word lists, and routines.

To order your copies, visit corwin.com/literacy

At Corwin Literacy we have put together a collection of just-in-time, classroom-tested, practical resources from trusted experts that allow you to quickly find the information you need when you need it.

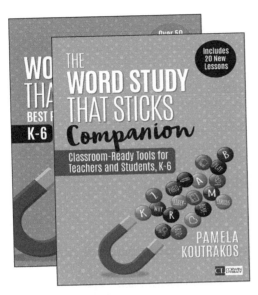

PAMELA KOUTRAKOS
Word Study That Sticks and its resource companion deliver challenging, discovery-based word learning routines and planning frameworks you can implement across subject areas.

MARIA WALTHER
101 picture-book experiences, a thousand ways to savor strategically. This is the book that shows how to use ANY book to teach readers and writers.

DOUGLAS FISHER, NANCY FREY, AND JOHN HATTIE
Ensure students demonstrate more than a year's worth of learning during a school year by implementing the right literacy practice at the right moment.

DOUGLAS FISHER, NANCY FREY, AND JOHN HATTIE
High-impact strategies to use for all you teach—all in one place. Deliver sustained, comprehensive literacy experiences to K–5 learners each day.

A SAGE Publishing Company

Helping educators make the greatest impact

CORWIN HAS ONE MISSION: to enhance education through intentional professional learning.

We build long-term relationships with our authors, educators, clients, and associations who partner with us to develop and continuously improve the best evidence-based practices that establish and support lifelong learning.